D0571148

DICTIONARY
OF WORD AND
PHRASE ORIGINS

Martin H. Manser

SPHERE BOOKS LIMITED

A SPHERE BOOK

First published in Great Britain by Sphere Books Ltd 1990
1st reprint 1990

Copyright © Martin H. Manser 1990

Printed and bound in Great Britain by
Cox & Wyman Ltd, Reading

ISBN 07474 0423 2

Sphere Books Ltd
A Division of
Macdonald & Co (Publishers) Ltd
Orbit House
1 New Fetter Lane
London EC4A 1AR

A member of Maxwell Macmillan Pergamon Publishing Corporation

To Hannah and Benjamin

Contents

INTRODUCTION

Why do we describe something as a **red herring**? Why is someone's behaviour said to be **beyond the pale**? What is the original meaning of the word **treacle**? This book explores the intriguing origins and development of about 800 words and expressions in English.

The entries in this dictionary are arranged in alphabetical order of the main word, except for some phrases that begin with a very common verb such as *get* or *make*. In these cases, the expressions are entered under the next main word, e.g. *get someone's goat* is included at GOAT. An index at the back of the book lists all the entries.

The articles about words named after people first appeared in my *Dictionary of Eponyms* (also published by Sphere Books). Some of the remaining material is an adaptation of part of my *Guinness Book of Words*. I also wish to express my appreciation of Mrs Rosalind Desmond for her painstaking typing and research help.

The story of the development of English provides an endless source of fascination not only for mother-tongue users but also for students of English as a foreign or second language. I hope therefore that something of the rich heritage of the language will be discovered and enjoyed in these pages.

Martin H. Manser
September 1989

A

A-1

If something is *A-1*, it is in the best possible state. The term was originally an abbreviation in the *Register of Shipping* of the insurance company Lloyd's of London and was used to describe ships in first-class condition. As the Register noted: 'The character A denotes new ships, or ships renewed or restored. The stores of vessels are designated by the figures 1 and 2.' So A-1 meant that the hull was in excellent condition, as was all the ship's equipment.

A1 is combined with *OK* to give *A-OK*. The term was first used by Colonel John A. ('Shorty') Powers, a public relations officer of the National Aeronautics and Space Administration (NASA) at the splashdown of the first US suborbital flight in 1961. Powers was reporting the words of the US astronaut Alan B. Shepard that everything was working perfectly. See also OK.

aback (be taken aback)

Someone who is *taken aback* is very surprised or shocked, and has to stop for a moment. The expression comes from the language of sailing-ships. A ship was taken aback when a strong gust of wind suddenly blew the sails back against the mast, causing the ship to stop momentarily. Naturally the sailors were greatly surprised at the unexpected event – hence the modern meaning of the phrase.

abacus

In ancient Greece an *abacus* was a slab or tablet (Greek *abax*) covered with a thin layer of sand. Calculations were traced in the sand and could then be erased. Later, strings of pebbles (Latin *calculus*, pebble) were used for this purpose. Pebbles were moved backwards and forwards along grooves to make calculations. The wooden frame of beads on wires that we call an abacus probably originated in China more than 5000 years ago. See also CALCULATE.

abracadabra

The word *abracadabra* is used by magicians when they are performing conjuring tricks. The word goes back to the Greek *abrasadabra*, a 'charm word' used by members of the Basilides, a Gnostic sect, when seeking divine help. This word may in turn derive from *abrasax*, originally a charm or amulet made up of Greek letters, believed to have magical powers and, from the 2nd century AD, the deity worshipped by this Gnostic sect. The name contains the number 365, the number of heavens, and their spirits, that emanated from him.

An alternative explanation is that the word derives from the first letters of three Hebrew words: *Ab*, Father, *Ben*, Son, and *Acadsch*, Holy Spirit.

Achilles' heel

An *Achilles' heel* is a weakness, fault, or vulnerable spot in a person or thing that is otherwise strong: *The party knows that its group of political extremists might well be its Achilles' heel.* The expression derives from Greek mythology, when Thetis, the mother of Achilles, dipped him into the River Styx to make him invulnerable. His one weak spot was the heel by which Thetis had held him during the dipping and which had not

2

been touched by the water. It was during the siege of Troy that Achilles was mortally wounded by a poisoned arrow that was shot into his heel.

acid test

An *acid test* is a decisive way of proving whether something is true or valuable: *The acid test is not whether consumers like our new product, but whether they will actually buy it.* The expression derives from the use of nitric acid to prove whether a metal is gold or not. If the metal was not gold, the acid decomposed it, but if it was genuine, the gold remained undamaged.

add insult to injury

To *add insult to injury* is to offend someone further after one has already harmed him or her in some other way: *To add insult to injury, only a small amount of money was offered as compensation.* A version of this phrase originated in the fables of the Roman author Phaedrus (?15BC–50AD). He quoted a fable by Aesop in which a bald man swatted at a fly that had bitten him, missed the fly and hit himself on the head instead. The fly then comments, 'You wanted to kill me for a mere touch. What will you do to yourself, now that you have added insult to injury?' The phrase in English comes from the play *The Foundling* (1748) by the English author Edward Moore (1712–57): 'This is adding insult to injuries'.

adder

In Middle English the viper now known as an *adder* was a *naddre*. The words *a naddre* were run together so that people thought that the words were *an addre*. The first sound of the original word *naddre* was wrongly attributed to the preceding indefinite article *a*. Other instances of this 'wrong' shortening include *an apron*, originally *a napron* – like our modern *napkin* – and *an umpire*, originally *a noumpere*. The reverse process has also taken place: *a newt* is a 'wrong' version of *an ewt*, *a nickname* a 'wrong' version of *an ekename*.

aegis (under the aegis)

If something is done *under the aegis* of a person or institution, it has their support or backing. The origin of this expression lies in Greek mythology. *Aigis* is the Greek word for goatskin, in this instance the skin of the goat Amalthaea that suckled the Greek god Zeus in his infancy. Later, the skin was used to cover the shield of Zeus, and since this shield represented the power of this supreme Greek god, someone who acted under his aegis enjoyed the security of divine protection.

aftermath

If something happens in the *aftermath* of a war, flood, etc., it happens immediately after such a catastrophic or disastrous event. This use of the word is an extension of the word's literal meaning. A *math* is a crop of grass, and so an *aftermath* is a second crop of grass mowed in the same season.

agnostic

It is rare that the coining of a word can be exactly dated and attributed to one individual, but this is the case with the word *agnostic*. The word was created by the English biologist Thomas Henry Huxley (1825–95), who was a leading British exponent of Darwin's theory of evolution. Huxley coined the word in 1869 when a member of the Metaphysical Society. He wanted a word to describe someone who would neither acknowledge nor reject the existence of a God, since he considered that such a matter could not be proved. Believing that nothing was knowable beyond the material, Huxley combined the Greek *a* (not) with *gignōskein* (to know) to give the word *agnostic*. In modern use the meaning of the word has changed slightly: an agnostic is someone who doubts the existence of God (rather than Huxley's original sense of someone who believes that the existence of God is not knowable) or, more generally, someone who is sceptical about a certain matter.

agony

Agony, meaning extreme mental or physical pain, comes from Greek *agōnia*, contest, particularly an athletic contest. *Agōnia* itself comes from *agōn*, the arena or stadium where the contests took place. Since each contest was a fight between competitors, the word *agōnia* came to refer to any struggle and from this came the sense of mental anguish.

aisle

An *aisle* is the passageway between areas of seating in a church, theatre, etc. The 14th-century English word was originally *ele*, borrowed from French and ultimately from Latin *ala*, meaning a wing or the part on either side of the nave of the church. The spelling of the word in English became changed to *aisle*, however, through confusion with the English word *isle*, an island, and under the influence of French *aile*, wing, and *allée*, alley. The English word also acquired the additional sense of passageway.

alarm

Alarm is a feeling of fear caused by an awareness of danger (*The radiation leak caused great alarm*) and a device that gives a warning signal (*sound the alarm*). The word comes from the Italian *all'arme*, to arms!, the call to equip oneself with weapons in preparation for battle.

alligator

When the Spanish first came across the alligator in their travels in the New World, they called this creature *el lagarto*, the lizard, because of its lizard-like characteristics. When the word was taken over into English, the two words *el lagarto* were thought to make up one single word – hence our term *alligator*.

ambition

Ambition is the strong desire to achieve success, to become rich, powerful, famous, etc. The origin of the word is Latin *ambitio*, going around. The word originally referred to the going around of political candidates from place to place, wooing potential voters. Today's ambitious entrepreneurs know something of this 'doing the rounds' in following up contacts in search of business.

ambulance

Until comparatively recent times, soldiers injured in battle were likely to remain where they fell until the end of the battle or until nightfall. In the latter case, medical aid would reach the wounded under the cover of darkness. Towards the end of the 18th century, however, the French army introduced a speedier method of bringing help to the injured – a vehicle equipped with bandages, tourniquets, etc., that could carry the wounded to hospital. This vehicle was known as a *hôpital ambulant*, walking hospital, from Latin *ambulare*, to walk. These mobile hospitals moved so quickly that they soon became known as *ambulances volantes*, flying walkers. It was when the British soldiers adopted the use of such vehicles that the name was shortened to *ambulance*.

amethyst

An *amethyst* is a purple stone that is used in making jewellery. The origin of the word shows that it was once considered extremely precious. The word comes from Latin *amethystus*, which in turn derives from Greek *amethystos*, a remedy against drunkenness, from *a*, not and *methyein*, to be drunk. Thus, goblets made of amethyst were thought to prevent intoxication, no matter how much wine was drunk.

ampersand

Ampersand is the name of the symbol &, meaning and. This sign once followed the alphabet in children's learning-books. Children would recite the name of the letters of the alphabet and then, to describe &, would say, 'and per se and', *per se* being Latin for 'by itself'. In time *and per se and* gradually became changed to our word *ampersand*.

antimacassar

In the 19th century, hair lotion was introduced that contained a large amount of macassar oil – a preparation whose ingredients were said to have come originally from *Makasar* (now Ujung Padang, in central Indonesia). The lotion was popular, Macassar even being used as the name of a proprietary brand. Hair so oiled, though, left a stain on the back of upholstered chairs, so the *antimacassar* (*anti*, against and *macassar*) was devised. This was a decorative cloth that could be put on the back of a chair to absorb the oil and keep the chair clean. Paper versions of the antimacassar are still used in some homes, railway carriages, and aeroplanes.

apple of one's eye

The *apple of one's eye* is a person whom one values as very precious. The expression comes from the Authorized (King James) Version of the Bible, Deuteronomy 32:10, describing God's tender love for his people: 'He found him in a desert land, and in the waste howling wilderness; he led him about, he instructed him, he kept him as the apple of his eye.'

The apple was originally a metaphor for the pupil of the eye, as an apple and a pupil are both round. The expression came to be applied to someone who was cherished greatly – as valuable to a person as his or her own eyes.

apple-pie order; apple-pie bed

The phrase *in apple-pie order*, meaning neat and tidy, had originally nothing to do with apples or pies. The expression comes from the French *nappe pliée*, folded linen, applied to table napkins and then more generally to other things that are neatly laid out in an ordered manner.

The practical joke an *apple-pie bed* is a bed made in such a way that someone cannot get into it. The origin of the expression may also lie in the French *nappe pliée*, as in *apple-pie order*. Other authorities suggest that the *pie* is a rough synonym of *turnover* – since a turnover is made by folding half a pastry crust over the other half, just as an apple-pie bed is made by doubling up a sheet.

arena

An *arena* is an area, usually enclosed, that is used for sports events and entertainments. The word is often also used in an applied sense to mean a sphere of activity: *in the political arena*. The origin of the word goes back to Roman times, when gladiators fought in the amphitheatre and crowds gathered to see bloodshed. To soak up the blood spilt when the fighters were in combat, the ground was liberally strewn with sand. It was by this sand that the place of fighting became known, *arena* being Latin for sand.

argosy

An *argosy*, a large merchant ship, particularly one carrying valuables, is named after the Dalmatian port of *Ragusa* (now Dubrovnik in Yugoslavia), where the ships were first built. The word came into English in the 16th century, via Italian *ragusea*, Ragusan (ship).

arrant

The word *arrant* is used to emphasize that something or someone is very bad: *what arrant nonsense; you arrant liar!* The word was formerly a variant of *errant*, wandering. In medieval times a *knight errant* was a young knight who roamed the countryside seeking to undertake acts of chivalry. Similarly, an *arrant thief* was a vagabond who wandered through the countryside robbing people. In time, *arrant* lost its meaning of 'wandering', and became an adjective of degree, to give its present meaning of 'utter, unmitigated, or notorious'.

arrowroot

Arrowroot is a starch obtained from a West Indian plant *Maranta arundinacea*, that is used in cooking. The plant was originally used by American Indians to heal wounds caused by poisoned arrows: tubers of the plant absorbed the poison. But although the name *arrowroot* describes the plant's medicinal properties, the real origin of the word may in fact lie in its native name *aru-aru*.

artesian well

An *artesian well* is a well in which the water is forced to the surface by natural pressure. Rainwater collects underground and cannot escape; as more water gathers, the pressure builds up and sends the water to the surface if a hole is bored down to it. The name of this type of well comes from *Arteis*, the Old French name for *Artois*, a former province in northern France where such wells were common.

the Ashes

When the England cricket team was beaten by Australia in 1882, a mock obituary notice was published in the *Sporting Times* of 2 September: 'In Affectionate Remembrance of English Cricket Which died at the Oval on 29th August, 1882. Deeply lamented by a large circle of sorrowing friends and acquaintances. R.I.P. N.B. – The body will be cremated and the ashes taken to Australia.' When England won the series of 1882–83 in Australia, the English team were presented with an urn containing the real ashes of a set of bails. The urn is kept at Lord's cricket ground in London. Nowadays, *the Ashes* stands for the trophy played for in a series of test matches between England and Australia; though even if Australia wins the series, the Ashes remain in England.

asparagus

Foreign words that are unfamiliar to mother-tongue speakers have been particularly vulnerable to the influence of what is known as folk etymology. Folk etymology means that unfamiliar words are replaced by more familiar, recognizable words. *Asparagus* is a well-known example of this influence. Although the word comes from Greek *asparagos*, it developed the dialectal form *sparrow-grass*, as if this plant were eaten by sparrows.

assassin

The word *assassin*, someone who kills a prominent person, especially for political motives, was used to refer to a member of a secret fanatical Muslim sect that operated in Persia and Syria in the 11th and 12th centuries. The sect was infamous for its campaign of terror in attempting to dominate the Muslim world. The name of the sect of Assassins further derives from Arabic *hashshāshīn*, hashish eaters, as it is commonly believed that they ate or smoked hashish before being sent to carry out their evil deeds.

Other words from Arabic that have come into English include: *alcohol, algebra, cipher, zenith* and *zero*.

atlas

In Greek mythology, Atlas was one of the Titans. As a punishment for his part in the attempt to overthrow Zeus, he was condemned to support the heavens on his shoulders for the rest of his life. The word *atlas* came to be used to refer to a book of maps after a drawing of *Atlas* was included in the title-page of a collection of maps by the map-maker Mercantor, published in the late 16th century.

In architecture, an *atlas* (plural, *atlantes*) is the male stone figure used as a column to support the entablature of a building. Female figures are known as *caryatids* or *caryatides*, from Greek *Karyatides*, the priestesses of the goddess Artemis at Caryae in Greece.

atone

To *atone* means to show that one is sorry for some wrongdoing and to do something to make things better. The origin of *atone* is the noun *atonement*, a 16th-century word coined to express the state of being 'at one' (*at-one-ment*), in the sense of being reconciled to God. From this concept of reconciliation came the idea of making amends for a wrong that had been committed.

augur

If something *augurs* well for someone, it is a sign of something good happening in the future. The origin of this verb lies in the Latin noun *augur*, a diviner. In ancient Rome an augur was an official whose responsibility it was to observe and interpret accepted signs and omens and so give guidance in the making of decisions. See AUSPICES.

auspices (*under the auspices of*)

If something is done *under the auspices of* an organization, it has that organization's guidance, help, and support. The word goes back to Roman times when an *augur* or *auspex*, a soothsayer or diviner, used to forecast the future by carefully studying the flight of birds – the direction of flight, their songs in flight, etc. – in the sky. Signs on the augur's left were favourable, those on his right unfavourable. *Auspices* derives from Latin *avis*, a bird and *specere*, to see.

An example of the alleged danger of ignoring the warnings of the auspices was that of the consul Gaius Flaminius. Ridiculing the clear signs of the omens, Flaminius marched against Hannibal but only hours later was defeated by him and killed at Lake Trasimene (217 BC).

axe (*have an axe to grind*)

If someone has an axe to grind, he or she has an interest or purpose, usually selfishly motivated, in helping a person or in doing something. The expression is said to come from a story *Too Much For Your Whistle* by Benjamin Franklin. Pretending that he didn't know how a grindstone worked, a stranger asked the young Franklin to show him. Franklin obliged, the man putting his axe to the grindstone as the boy energetically turned the wheel. When the axe was sharp, the man had achieved his purpose and so just laughed at the boy and walked away. More happily, the phrase nowadays is usually used in the negative rather than in the positive: *Since she's got no particular axe to grind, she's standing for election as an Independent.*

B

babel

A *babel* is a noisy confusion of sounds or voices. The expression comes from the biblical tower of *Babel* (probably, Babylon), built with the intention of reaching to heaven (Genesis 11:1–9). God confounded the builders' efforts by causing them to speak different languages so that they could not understand one another, and scattering them throughout the earth.

babes in the wood

If people are described as *babes in the wood*, they are thought to be very inexperienced and innocent, unaware of the wicked circumstances around them. The expression *babes in the wood* is the popular title of the late 16th-century story *The Children in the Wood*.

In the tale, a wealthy Norfolk gentleman dies, leaving his property to his infant son and daughter. Until the children are old enough to inherit the property, they are to be looked after by their uncle. If they die before they reach such an age, however, the uncle is to acquire the estate. The temptation proves too strong for the wicked uncle, who hires two ruffians to kill the children in a wood. One of the men is tender-hearted and cannot bring himself to kill the children, so kills his fellow assassin instead and leaves the children to look after themselves in the wood. They die in the night, unable to survive the cruel environment and a robin covers their bodies over with leaves. The wicked uncle then suffers all kinds of calamities; the surviving thug is arrested and later confesses – and the whole truth of the wicked plot comes out.

bacon (bring home the bacon)

The idiomatic expression *bring home the bacon* has two meanings – to be the person in a family who provides money, food, etc., and to be successful in achieving something.

Some authorities suggest that the origin of this phrase is the winning of the prize of a greased pig at a traditional country fair. An alternative explanation, offered by other authorities, describes the tradition of Great Dunmow, Essex, in England, known as the Dunmow Flitch. According to this custom, which goes back to 1111, a married couple who can prove that they have lived for a year and a day without quarrelling or wishing to be unmarried, are presented with a flitch or a side of bacon. The Dunmow Flitch mock trial is still held every four years.

baffle

If something *baffles* you, it puzzles you and you cannot understand it. The origin of the word may lie in the language of chivalry, when it meant to disgrace publicly. In medieval times if a knight had acted dishonourably, he would by hung up by the heels and taunted with his misdeeds. Occasionally, a picture of the disgraced knight in such a position was hung up instead. This treatment was known as being baffled.

baker's dozen

A *baker's dozen* is 13. The expression probably dates back to a baking practice in 15th-century England, when, so it is said, bakers had a reputation for selling underweight bread. Stringent regulations were therefore introduced, establishing weights for different types of bread. So, to be on the safe side and to avoid possible heavy fines, bakers cooked 13 – not 12 – loaves in a batch of a dozen, in order to satisfy the standard weight regulations.

the balloon goes up

When the balloon goes up describes the beginning of an important activity. The origin of the phrase lies in the barrage balloons used in the two world wars to deter low-flying enemy aircraft. The fact that these balloons had been raised meant that an attack was imminent – hence the contemporary application of the expression.

ballot

The term ballot, meaning a secret vote, is derived from Italian ballotta, little ball. It is so called because in early times casting a vote was carried out by secretly dropping a small ball into a container. White and black balls were used – white meaning 'for' and black 'against'. This practice led also to the use of the verb blackball, to prevent someone from joining a group, club, etc.

bandy

If you bandy words with someone, you quarrel with him or her. The word comes from French, and its original meaning was 'to hit the ball backwards and forwards' in an early form of tennis. So from the sporting exchange of a ball has come the quarrelsome exchange of words. In modern English, the phrase is often used in the negative: *I'm not going to bandy words with you*, means, in effect, let's not waste time arguing.

bankrupt

A moneylender in medieval Italy worked from a *banca*, a bench or shelf. When he was no longer able to continue in business because of a shortage of funds, his bench was broken up and he was referred to as *bancarotta*, literally 'bench broken'. From this, the word *bankrupt* gradually came to be used for an insolvent person, someone whom a court has declared unable to pay his or her debts.

bark up the wrong tree

If you say that someone is *barking up the wrong tree*, you mean that he or she is directing attention, enquiries, etc., towards the wrong person or thing. The phrase is said to derive from 19th-century raccoon hunting. Such hunting took place at night, with hunters depending on their dogs to chase a raccoon up a tree. The dogs then lay in wait at the foot of the tree and barked until the hunters came. Obviously a dog that was barking up the wrong tree was mistaken and was wasting its efforts, and so the modern application of the expression.

barnacle

A *barnacle* is a sea animal with a hard shell, specifically one that lives attached to rocks, the hulls of ships, etc. There is also the *barnacle goose*, the Arctic goose with a black neck and grey wings. The English word *barnacle* was first applied only to the bird, and it was some three centuries later, in the 16th century, that the word was applied to the shellfish. In medieval times, as one curious theory has it, the two were thought to be different forms of the same creature. The shellfish was thought to have grown on a tree on the seashore and to have been able to generate this species of goose. It is also possible, however, that the names for the two creatures are derived independently from different sources.

batty

If someone is described as batty, he or she is considered eccentric or slightly mad. The word probably comes from the phrase *have bats in one's belfry*, thought to have been first used by Ambrose Bierce in the early 20th century. The expression alludes to the bats living in a bell-tower. When the bells ring, the bats fly about wildly – just as the thoughts of a mad person do in his or her disturbed mind.

be-all and end-all

The *be-all and end-all* of something is the most important element or purpose of something. The expression derives from Shakespeare's *Macbeth* (Act 1, Scene vii):

> ... that but this blow
> Might be the be-all and the end-all here,
> But here, upon this bank and shoal of time,
> We'd jump the life to come.

bead

A *bead* is a small ball. The word comes from an Old English word meaning a prayer. The change of meaning came about because of the religious practice of keeping up with the number of prayers to be said. The means of counting such prayers was the rosary with its small balls, and praying with the rosary was known as *telling* or *counting one's beads*. In the course of time, the word bead came to stand for the small counting ball used in praying as well as for the prayer itself. Bead has now lost the meaning 'prayer', but its range of meanings has been extended to include other small round shapes, for example beads of sweat. Interestingly, the related German word, *beten*, still means 'to pray'.

beam (on one's beam ends)

If someone is *on his or her beam-ends*, he or she has no money left to live on. The phrase derives from a former nautical term. The beams were the horizontal timbers of a wooden sailing-ship that supported the deck and held the sides in place. So if a ship was on its beam-ends, these timbers would be standing vertically instead of lying in a horizontal position, and the ship would be nearly capsizing – in a desperate situation indeed.

beat about the bush

If someone *beats about the bush*, he or she avoids talking about the main point of a matter. The phrase derives from the language of huntsmen. Hunters used to employ beaters who beat bushes in order to startle the game birds into the air – the hunters could then shoot at the birds in flight. So, unlike the beaters the hunter was not one to beat about the bush but someone who got directly to the point.

because it's there

Because it's there was the reply given in 1923 by the mountain-eer George Mallory when asked by a New York newspaper reporter why he wanted to climb Mount Everest. Mallory made two unsuccessful attempts to climb Everest, in 1922 and 1924. On the second attempt he and a companion vanished from sight on the mountain; it is not known whether they succeeded in reaching the summit before they died.

The quotation *because it's there* is sometimes attributed to others, notably Sir Edmund Hillary, who succeeded in conquering Mount Everest in 1953.

bed (*get out of bed on the wrong side*)

This expression is used to describe someone who seems bad-tempered, or for whom everything appears to go wrong. The phrase has its origins in the superstition that left is unlucky and right is lucky. The superstition was that if you put your left leg out of bed first, you would be unlucky. The day would therefore be spoiled even before it had really started. No wonder, then, that you would be bad-tempered for the rest of the day.

bedlam

The word *bedlam*, meaning a noisy confusion, is an alteration of the word *Bethlehem*. This in turn is short for the Hospital of St Mary of *Bethlehem*, the name of a London priory, founded in 1247, that was converted into a lunatic asylum in the 16th century. The word bedlam was first used for such asylums in general, and then later for the uproar that might be seen in them. The hospital has moved within London and is now the Bethlem Royal Hospital at Beckenham, Kent, and part of the Maudsley (psychiatric) Hospital.

bee (have a bee in one's bonnet; the bee's knees; make a beeline)

Someone who *has a bee in his or her bonnet* about something is so enthusiastic about a subject that he or she cannot talk about anything else. The expression is said to derive from the strange behaviour that follows from having a bee trapped under one's hat: a person in such a predicament clearly is obsessed with the bee and can think about nothing else.

The phrase *bee's knees* is used to describe someone who thinks he or she is superior or clever: *She thinks she's the bee's knees*. The expression may derive from the supposed careful bending of the knees as bees remove pollen from their bodies to put it in their pollen sacs, or, more simply, from the rhyming of the words *bees* and *knees* chosen apparently arbitrarily.

To make a beeline for someone or something is to go directly towards them, especially in a straight line. The expression derives from the belief that bees return in a straight line towards their hive, having collected nectar from flowers.

beefeater

The yeoman warders of the Tower of London are known colloquially as *beefeaters*. Why? In the late 15th century, when the royal bodyguard was appointed, *eater* meant 'servant', and *beef* was an indication of a high status and an advanced standard of living. In comparison with the more menial servants – formerly known as loaf-eaters – the beef-servants or *beefeaters* enjoyed a more comfortable way of life.

According to a less likely theory, the word derives from *buffetier*, a favoured servant whose job was to attend the royal *buffet* or sideboard.

beggar

You might think that the word *beggar* derives simply from the verb to *beg*, but it is quite possible that this is not the case. The word may well derive from the nickname of Lambert Le *Bègue* (Lambert the Stammerer), a 12th-century Belgian priest who founded a religious order for women in Liège. The nuns were known as *Beguines*. They lived a semi-religious, austere communal life but were not required to take vows and were allowed to own property and also to leave the community. Later, a similar order was established for men, known as *Beghards*, but they had communal funds and were not allowed to own private property. It seems that others posed as members of the male religious order, asking for alms, bringing the order into low esteem. The word, it appears, remained and the *Beghards* in time became the *beggars*.

beggar description

If something *beggars description*, it is impossible to describe, because it is extraordinarily beautiful, unusual, etc: *The calmness of the sea in the evening light beggared all description*. The expression derives from Shakespeare's *Antony and Cleopatra* (Act 2, Scene ii) in the speech of Enobarbus, Antony's friend:

> The barge she sat in, like a burnish'd throne,
> Burn'd on the water; the poop was beaten gold,
> Purple the sails, and so perfumed, that
> The winds were love-sick with them, the oars were silver,
> Which to the tune of flutes kept stroke, and made
> The water which they beat to follow faster,
> As amorous of their strokes. For her own person,
> It beggar'd all description ...

belfry

A *belfry* is a church steeple, especially one in which bells are hung. The word comes from Middle French *berfrei*, a medieval movable siege-tower that was pushed up to the walls of a city so that missiles could be thrown down upon the city's inhabitants. It seems that church steeples are called belfries because of their resemblance to these towers.

bell, book, and candle

Bell, book, and candle describes the instruments formerly used in the ceremony of excommunication from the Roman Catholic Church. A bell was rung, the book closed and candle extinguished – to express the lasting spiritual darkness to which the person was condemned. The expression is sometimes used to refer also to inordinately elaborate ritual.

bell the cat

To *bell the cat* means to take a risk or do something dangerous in order to benefit others. This rather dated expression has its origins in an old fable. A group of mice held a meeting to decide what to do about a cat who was troubling them all greatly. One wise mouse suggested that a bell should be hung round the cat's neck to warn them of the cat's approach. All the mice agreed that this was a good idea but, as one mouse put it, 'Who will bell the cat?'

belt (below the belt)

Actions or remarks that are *below the belt* are unfair and also sometimes unscrupulous or cowardly: *That last comment was a bit below the belt.* The phrase comes from the Queensberry rules for boxing, established by John Sholto Douglas, the 8th Marquis of Queensberry (1844–1900), and published in 1867. According to these rules, a blow struck to an opponent below the belt of his shorts – i.e. one dealt in the groin – is regarded as foul play.

berserk (go berserk)

If someone *goes berserk*, he or she goes into a state of wild or violent fury: *A young man shot five children in a playground this morning and then ended up shooting himself; he is believed to have gone berserk.* The word *berserk* is derived from Old Norse *berserkr*, from *bern*, a bear, and *serkr*, a shirt or coat. A *berserkr* was an extraordinary wild Viking warrior, so demented with battle frenzy that he would rush into battle without weapons of any sort and clothed only in a bearskin.

best bib and tucker

One's *best bib and tucker* means one's finest clothes. The phrase, first used in the late 16th century, originated in the clothes worn by a couple dressing up for a special occasion. The man wore a *bib*-front to his shirt to keep it clean, and the woman wore a *tucker*, a piece of fine lace or muslin tucked around the neck of her dress. So a couple in their best *bib and tucker* were smartly dressed for that important social occasion.

the best-laid schemes of mice and men

The saying *the best-laid schemes of mice and men* is sometimes used when, despite careful planning, something goes wrong. The phrase is a quotation from the poem *To a Mouse* by Robert Burns:

The best laid schemes o' mice an' men
Gang aft agley

24

beware the Greeks bearing gifts

Beware the Greeks bearing gifts is a saying advising suspicion of presents or benefits that are offered because they could possibly be dangerous. The expression comes from a line in Virgil's *Aeneid*: *Timeo Danaos et dona ferentes* ('I fear the Greeks, even when they bring gifts'). The allusion is to the famous Greek gift of the Trojan horse. Having laid siege to Troy for ten years without success, the Greeks ostensibly indicated that they were ready to retreat. As they prepared to return home, they presented a gift of a large hollow wooden horse to the Trojans. Although advised to 'beware the Greeks even when they bring gifts', the horse was taken into the city, whereupon Greek soldiers emerged and launched their final assault on Troy.

Big Ben

Big Ben is not, as is commonly supposed, the clock in the tower of the Houses of Parliament (the Palace of Westminster), London, but is the name of the bell itself. The bell, cast from 1856–58 and weighing 13½ tons, is named after Sir *Benjamin* Hall (1802–67), First Commissioner of Works at the time. The hours are struck on Big Ben; the sound of Big Ben striking, first broadcast in 1923, has become well known throughout the world.

big brother

Big brother is the title of the sinister all-powerful leader of the totalitarian state in the novel *1984* by George Orwell, published in 1949. The expression has passed into the language to refer to the all-pervasive presence of a ruthless and dictatorial person, organization, or system. The phrase occurs most commonly in the expression *Big brother is watching you*, said for example when commenting on the apparent invasion of privacy by modern computerized technology.

bikini

The word *bikini*, for a woman's brief two-piece swimming–costume, comes from *Bikini*, an atoll in the Marshall Islands in the Pacific and the site of atomic-bomb tests in 1946. The sensational effects of wearing the beachwear – designed in France the following year – were compared to the explosive power of the atomic bomb, and hence the name.

Biro

Biro is a trademark used to describe a kind of ballpoint pen. It is named after its Hungarian-born inventor László Jozsef *Biró* (1900–85). Biró patented his ballpoint pen, containing quick-drying ink, in Hungary in 1938. The rise of Nazism meant that Biró left Hungary, and settled in Argentina.

Biró's pen soon proved popular: for instance, Royal Air Force navigators found that it wrote better at high altitudes than a conventional fountain pen.

Towards the end of World War II, Biró found an English company who backed his product, but the company was soon taken over by the French firm Bic. So it is that the ballpoint pen is known in France as a bic and in the UK as a biro.

biscuit

Biscuits, small thin dry pieces of pastry that have been baked, were originally cooked twice so that they would not spoil during long sea voyages. Thus the word *biscuit* comes from the French (*pain*) *bescuit*, twice-cooked (bread). The firing of earthenware or porcelain before glazing is also known by this term.

bite the bullet; bite the dust; bite the hand that feeds one

To *bite the bullet* means to face an unpleasant experience with courage. The expression probably comes from medicine. In the 19th century, surgeons often had to operate on wounded soldiers without the aid of an anaesthetic. The patient was given a bullet and was urged to bite on it, in order to distract his attention from the pain.

To *bite the dust* is to fall from one's horse to the ground, die, or, figuratively, stop functioning or suffer a severe failure. Typically, westerns consist solely of American Indians biting the dust. The phrase is a virtual translation of a line in Homer's *Iliad*, translated by the US poet William Cullen Bryant (1794–1878): 'His fellow warriors, many a one, Fall round him to the earth and bite the dust'.

To *bite the hand that feeds one* means to be ungrateful towards or to insult someone to whom one should be thankful. The British political theorist Edmund Burke (1729–97)) may have been one of the first to use this expression. In an essay published posthumously, he wrote: 'And having looked to government for bread, on the very first scarcity they will turn and bite the hand that fed them.'

bitter (to the bitter end)

The phrase *to the bitter end*, means to the very end; until death or ultimate defeat: *Our team were losing, but we felt we had to stay and watch the game to the bitter end*. The phrase has a nautical background: the anchor ropes and cables on early sailing-ships were wound round a post, called the *bitt*, on the deck. The parts of the ropes nearest to the bitts were the bitter ends. If the rope were unwound to the bitter end, to the final part of the rope, a ship would be much more likely to suffer shipwreck or other calamity. Thus, the grim meaning of the expression.

black (in someone's black books; black sheep)

If you are *in someone's black books*, you are out of favour with him or her and liable to receive punishment: *He's been in the teacher's black books since he was caught cheating in the exams*. The first well-known black book was compiled by Henry VIII in his campaign against the Catholic Church. Henry VIII compiled a list of English monasteries and alleged abuses in them. This later resulted in the Crown taking possession of the monasteries' lands. In due course, the army, police and universities began to compile lists of those who were out of favour or deserved punishment in black books, and so the meaning of the expression became generally current.

Someone who is a *black sheep* is a member of a group who has failed in some respect: *There's a black sheep in every family*. The saying arose because shepherds disliked black sheep since their fleece was not worth anything, and believed that black sheep frightened the other sheep. In the course of time, the expression came to be applied to disgraced people.

blackmail

It might be thought that the word *blackmail*, threatening to do something such as revealing a secret about a person unless money is handed over, has something to do with the postal service, but this is not so. *Mail* here means rent or tax and *black* has the figurative sense 'wicked'. The word originates in Scotland: bandits along the Scotland/England border demanded blackmail – money paid as the price for free passage and protection from harm.

blarney

Blarney is smooth and flattering, but perhaps insincere, talk. The word comes from the legend that anyone who kisses the Blarney Stone, in *Blarney* Castle, near Cork in the Republic of Ireland will be given the skill to speak flattering language.

The probable origin of the use of this word lies in the story of McCarthy Mor, the lord of Blarney Castle, who in 1602 was defeated by the British led by Sir George Carew. McCarthy agreed to surrender but, it is said, put off for months the actual event of submission by giving one excuse after another. The continual delay meant that Carew became the target for jokes in the royal court, and *blarney* came to stand for smooth persuasive speech.

blaze a trail

If someone *blazes a trail,* he or she is discovering or exploring something exciting. The phrase comes from the time when explorers marked out a trail by chipping part of the bark off a tree. The resulting bare wood was known as a *blaze.* In this way, the route could be easily followed by those who came later. Today the expression is used in a figurative sense, and the derived noun *trailblazer* means a pioneer.

the blind leading the blind

If a situation is described as an instance of *the blind leading the blind,* people who are inexperienced or ignorant are trying to help or direct others who are themselves inexperienced or ignorant. The result is that neither group is helped. The expression comes from the words of Jesus, as recorded in the Authorized (King James) Version of the Bible, Matthew 15:14, describing the Pharisees: 'They be blind leaders of the blind. And if the blind lead the blind, both shall fall into the ditch.'

blitz

Blitz is German for 'lightning' and joined with *Krieg*, war, it was used to describe Hitler's military campaigns. A *blitzkrieg*, a sudden attack that is designed to defeat the enemy quickly, became shortened to *blitz*, and this word was used in particular to describe the heavy bombing of British cities by the Luftwaffe in 1940–41. *Blitz* is now also used in an extended sense to refer to a sudden intensive effort to get something done: *We'll have a blitz on the garden and get it all tidied up today.*

bloomers

Bloomers are a kind of women's undergarment that has full loose legs gathered at the knee. The word owes its origin to the US feminist Amelia Jenks *Bloomer* (1818–94), but the garment Bloomer introduced into American society was not the garment known as bloomers today. The original garment was an entire costume consisting of a loose-fitting tunic, a short knee-length skirt, and billowing Turkish-style trousers gathered by elastic at the ankle. The costume, designed originally by Elizabeth Smith Miller, and worn by Mrs Bloomer, was introduced at a ball in Lowell, Massachusetts, in July 1851. The outfit aroused considerable controversy at the time, largely because it was thought that trousers were a garment to be worn only by men. Later, bloomers came to refer to just the trousers in the outfit, towards the end of the 19th century, to knee-length knickerbockers worn by cyclists, and today, in somewhat informal and old-fashioned usage, to a variety of women's underwear.

blow hot and cold

If someone *blows hot and cold* he or she alternates between being very keen on something and having no interest in it at all. The expression comes from one of Aesop's fables, in which a satyr met a traveller in a wood in winter. The traveller was blowing on his fingers to get them warm. The satyr invited the traveller to his home for refreshment and gave him a bowl of hot soup. The man then started blowing again – this time to cool the soup. Alarmed, the satyr ejected the man, exclaiming that he did not want to have anything to do with someone who could 'blow hot and cold from the same mouth'.

blue (blue-blooded; blue-chip; once in a blue moon)

Someone who has *blue blood* or is *blue-blooded* belongs to a royal or aristocratic family. The expression is a translation of Spanish *sangre azul*, referring originally to Spaniards who had no Moorish ancestry but were pure Spanish. Such Spanish nobles had fairer complexions than the dark-skinned Moors and so the blood in their veins appeared blue.

A *blue-chip* investment or business firm is one that is thought to be reliable and profitable. The expression comes from gambling games such as poker. Chips or counters vary in value from red, the cheapest, to blue, the most valuable. So a *blue-chip* investment is one that is likely to give the highest return.

The expression *once in a blue moon*, meaning very rarely, seems to have its origins in a very old proverb, first recorded in print in 1528:

Yf they say the mone is blewe
We must believe that it is true.

This saying meant that no one really believed that the moon was blue – so *once in a blue moon* meant never. The change to its present meaning of very rarely seems to have come about because owing to certain atmospheric conditions the moon very occasionally does appear to have a slight tinge of blue.

blurb

A *blurb* is a short publicity notice, especially on a book cover. The word was coined in 1907 by the US humorist and illustrator Gelett Burgess (1866–1951) to promote his book *Are You a Bromide?*

In the early years of the 20th century, American novels commonly had a picture of an attractive young woman on the cover. In an effort to parody this practice, Burgess produced a picture of a sickly sweet girl, Miss Belinda *Blurb*, for the purpose, he hoped, of 'blurbing a blurb to end all blurbs'. The outstanding success of this example meant that the word became associated with all such publicity notes.

board (*above board; go by the board*)

An arrangement that is *above board* is done correctly and honestly. The expression derives from card playing and gambling: hands, cards, etc., were to be kept above the board or table, so that nothing deceptive or fraudulent could be carried out under the board.

The *boards* in the phrase *go by the board* were originally the sides of a sailing-ship. If a ship was in a heavy storm, and the ship's mast broke, the mast might go by the board – fall overboard or over the side – and be lost for ever. The expression is now used figuratively: if a plan goes by the board, then it is abandoned or discarded.

Bohemian

An artist or writer who lives an unconventional life, often in a community with others, may be known as a *Bohemian*. The word derives from *Bohemia*, a former kingdom of the Austrian empire in what is now Czechoslovakia, since it was thought that Bohemia was the home of the roaming vagabonds and gypsies found throughout Europe. The term became established when Thackeray described Becky Sharp, his headstrong heroine in *Vanity Fair* (1848), as: 'of a wild, roving nature, inherited from father and mother, who were both Bohemians by taste and circumstances'.

a bolt from the blue

Something that is a bolt from the blue is very unexpected and shocking: *News of the president's resignation came like a bolt from the blue.* A *bolt from the blue* refers to a sudden unexpected thunderclap and lightning streak from a cloudless blue sky.

bone (have a bone to pick; make no bones about something)

If *you have a bone to pick with someone*, you have a reason for a quarrel or complaint with someone and want to discuss matters with him or her. The expression has its origins in the fact that two dogs would in all probability fight over a single bone that was thrown to them.

To *make no bones about something* means not to hesitate about doing something difficult or unpleasant: *She made no bones about frankly criticizing the film in her article.* The expression may have originally referred to finding no bones in a bowl of soup that was served. The soup was therefore palatable and easy to swallow quickly, and so the phrase came to refer to something that was done straightforwardly. An alternative explanation is that the *bones* are dice. Some gamblers perform extravagant rituals with the dice before casting their throw in order to win good luck. Others *make no bones* about it, just shaking the dice once and throwing it.

the boot is on the other foot

If *the boot is on the other foot*, a situation has been reversed: *She used to have to obey my orders. The boot is now on the other foot and I have to do what she tells me.* The expression is said to have its origins in the times when footwear was made to fit either foot. (It was not until the 19th century that 'right' and 'left' shoes were introduced in volume.) So when a man tried on boots that didn't fit properly, his difficulty could often be overcome by changing the boots round. The situation had been totally reversed – the boot was now on the other foot.

boot (to boot)

The phrase *to boot* (besides) is added at the end of a further comment: *He's strong, sensitive, and good-looking to boot.* The word *boot* in this phrase has no connection with the article of footwear. Rather, it comes from the Old English word *bōt*, an advantage or remedy. In this meaning it was at one time used both as a verb (*What boots it?*) and adjective (*bootless*, futile), nowadays it remains only in the phrase *to boot*.

born with a silver spoon in one's mouth

If you say that someone was *born with a silver spoon in his or her mouth* you mean that that person was born into a very rich family. The expression derives from the old tradition of godparents giving their godchild a silver spoon at the baby's christening. The silver spoon therefore symbolized the child's good fortune from and in its birth.

borstal

A *borstal* is an institution in which young offenders are detained for corrective training. Known officially as a youth custody centre, the name borstal comes from the village of *Borstal*, Rochester, Kent, England, where the first institution was set up in 1902.

Boxing Day

Boxing Day, 26 December, is so called because in former times tradesman and employees were traditionally given a gift of money on that day. In medieval times, Boxing Day (St Stephen's Day) was the day on which alms-boxes in churches were opened and their contents divided amongst the poor. Nowadays, some people still give Christmas 'boxes' or gifts of money to tradesman, e.g. those delivering milk or newspapers, in gratitude for services rendered during the previous year, the gifts being given during the week before Christmas.

boycott

To *boycott* a person, organization, etc., means that one refuses to deal with them, as an expression of disapproval and often as a means of trying to force them to accept certain conditions. The word comes from the name of the Irish land-agent Captain Charles Cunningham *Boycott* (1832–97).

After retiring from the British army, Boycott was hired to look after the Earl of Erne's estates in County Mayo, Ireland. In 1880 the Irish Land League, wanting land reform, proposed a reduction in rents, stating that landlords who refused to accept such rents should be ostracized. Boycott refused and was promptly ostracized. His workers were forced to leave him, tradesman refused to supply him, and his wife was threatened – indeed he was persecuted to such a degree that he and his wife were forced to flee to England, in so doing making the first *boycott* a success.

brand-new

Something that is *brand-new* is completely new. The expression was applied originally to metal products that had just been taken from the *brand* (fire) of the forge in which they had been shaped. In modern German *Brand* means fire and the same phrase is used: *brandneu* for brand-new. In English, *brand* is still used in the sense of 'a piece of burning wood; a torch' in the phrase *a brand plucked* (or *snatched*) *from the burning*, a person who is rescued from a wrong way of life.

brass (get down to brass tacks)

To *get down to brass tacks* means to begin to discuss the basic important facts of a matter. A number of different suggestions have been made for the derivation of the phrase. The most likely theory is that the brass tacks were originally brass-headed nails, nailed onto the top of a counter in a store, and used to measure fabric by the yard. So after a customer had selected a material, the merchant would say, 'Let's get down to brass tacks,' and would measure the length of material required against the nails on the counter.

brave new world

Brave new world has become a catch-phrase to refer to a future ideal era brought about by great social reforms. The expression has its origins in Shakespeare's *The Tempest* (Act 5, Scene i);

> How many goodly creatures are there here!
> How beauteous mankind is! O brave new world,
> That has such people in't.

In contemporary usage, the phrase is commonly used in a derogatory sense, 'referring to the sterile uniformity and bureaucratization of modern life' (*The Facts on File Dictionary of Classical, Biblical, & Literary Allusions*). This usage derives from the novel *Brave New World* by English writer Aldous Huxley (1894–1964), published in 1932.

breach (once more unto the breach)

The rallying cry *once more unto the breach* is sometimes used in contemporary English when one is returning to a difficult task or situation. The origin of the expression is Shakespeare's *King Henry V* (Act 3, Scene i):

> Once more unto the breach, dear friends, once more;
> Or close the wall up with our English dead!

bread and circuses

Bread and circuses is the translation of a Latin phrase originally coined by the Roman satirical poet Juvenal (?60–?140AD). Describing the Romans, Juvenal wrote, 'Only two things limit their anxious longing – bread and the games of the circus.' In other words, the practice of feeding the people and providing them with entertainment at public expense keeps them satisfied with the government and so avoids any possible rebellion.

broke (go for broke)

To *go for broke* is to risk all that one has in the hope of gaining a great success. The phrase comes from gambling: if one puts all one's money on a single game or a single hand of cards, one is *going for broke*: if one loses, then one is completely broke – one has nothing; if one wins, one has everything.

browse

To *browse* means to look through a book, magazine, etc., in a casual way. The original meaning comes from the Old French *brost*, the young shoots, leaves, and twigs that animals such as deer and goats feed on. So *browse* has the sense of feeding on plant foliage, and, figuratively, of sampling things in a casual leisurely manner, e.g. reading short passages from a magazine, or looking round a shop in an unhurried way trying to find something interesting.

buccaneer

A *buccaneer* is a pirate, especially one who plundered the Spanish ships in the West Indies in the 17th and 18th centuries. The word comes from Old French *boucan*, a wooden frame for smoking meat, and ultimately from a word of Tupi origin. The name *buccaneer* was originally applied to French and English hunters in the West Indies who trapped and killed wild oxen and dried the meat of these animals on such frames. The name was later applied to Spanish pirates as their habits were similar to the French and English hunters. Nowadays the word *buccaneer* also sometimes refers to an unscrupulous business entrepreneur.

the buck stops here

A sign with the words *the buck stops here* was displayed on the White House desk of Harry S. Truman, US President from 1945–53. The reference is to the expression *pass the buck*, to shift responsibility. So the sign on the president's desk meant that the responsibility would not be passed on to others, but that he would accept ultimate liability.

The phrase *pass the buck*, originated in the game of poker. A buckhorn knife – a knife whose handle was made of a buck's horn – was formerly placed in front of the player whose turn it was to deal, and who also had the unwelcome task of betting the initial stake. So this player wanted to 'pass the buck', in other words wanted someone else to take the responsibility.

buff

The use of *buff* in the sense of enthusiast (*a movie buff, a word buff*) comes from the buff-coloured uniforms worn by volunteer firemen of New York City in the 19th century. They were so enthusiastic about going to fires that the word came to stand for any keen amateur fire-watcher and, in the course of time, to an expert in any subject.

A person who is *in the buff* is naked. *Buff* here was originally the undyed leather of the buffalo. Because of its light colour, the term was applied to describe bare human skin.

bungalow

The word *bungalow*, a one-storey house, is a borrowing from Hindi *banglā*, literally (a house) in the Bengali style. Other words that derive from Hindi include: *chutney, dinghy, dungarees, juggernaut, jungle, kedgeree, pundit*, and *shampoo*.

bunk

Bunk (or *bunkum*) is foolish nonsense. This expressive word comes from *Buncombe* County, North Carolina, USA. In 1820 Felix Walker, the County's congressional representative, made a long rambling speech in the House of Representatives. When asked to defend his action, Walker answered 'I am not speaking for your ears. I am only talking for Buncombe' – in other words, to impress his constituents. Walker's comment 'talking for Buncombe' was widely reported and came to mean to talk nonsense. The altered spelling *bunkum* and the shortened form *bunk* were popular by the mid-19th century.

burgle

If someone *burgles* a house, he or she breaks into the house and steals things. The verb *burgle* comes from the noun *burglar*, in other words it is a back formation – a word formed by removing an imagined suffix from a related familiar word. For example, a noun ending in *–ar*, *–er* or *–or* seems to be made up of an existing verb and the 'doer' ending. So *pedlar* and *editor* were falsely considered in this way to be derivatives of *peddle* and *edit*, which then came into use.

Other examples of back formation include: *commute* from *commuter*, *diagnose* from *diagnosis*, and *televise* from *television*.

burn one's boats/bridges

To *burn one's bridges* (or *boats*) is to act in such a way that makes retreat impossible. The expression originated with the Romans. Roman generals, e.g. Caesar, did at times burn all the Roman boats after invading foreign territory in order to strengthen the determination of his troops not to retreat. In time, bridges were burned for the same reason and the phrase came to have the figurative sense of committing oneself irrevocably to a particular course of action, allowing no means of escape whatsoever.

Burton (go for a Burton)

If something *goes for a Burton*, it is ruined or destroyed: *If you want me to do all that extra work, well, that's my weekend gone for a*

Burton. The expression originated during World War II: if an airman *went for a Burton*, he was killed or went missing while in action. There are a number of theories of the origin of the phrase, the most likely one being a reference to *Burton* ale, the name of a kind of strong beer, Burton-upon-Trent, in Staffordshire, England, being famous as a brewing town. It may well be that the original sense of the phrase *he's gone for a Burton* meant 'he's gone for a drink', a euphemistic reference to death. Alternatively, since *the drink* also refers to the sea, an airman shot down over the sea could have been said to have *gone for a Burton.*

bury the hatchet; bury one's head in the sand

If two opponents *bury the hatchet*, they settle an argument and become friendly again. The phrase derives from the American Indian tradition of taking the tomahawks and other weapons of the leaders of the warring groups – two tribes or the American Indians and the Whites – and literally burying the weapons in the ground. This was the sign that hostilities between the two groups were over and that peace had come. If hostilities broke out again, then the weapons were dug up as a sign that war had been declared.

To *bury one's head in the sand* is to refuse to notice a difficulty or problem or to avoid facing up to realities. The phrase alludes to the belief that the ostrich buries its head in the sand when it is being pursued. The ostrich supposedly does this in the belief that because it is unable to see its enemy, it itself cannot be seen.

busman's holiday

A *busman's holiday* is a holiday or a day off from work that is spent doing something similar to one's usual job. The phrase is said to originate in the early years of the 20th century when drivers of old London horse-buses were so fond of their horses that they spent their rest day as a passenger on their own bus – to make sure that the horses were properly looked after.

butter wouldn't melt in someone's mouth

The phrase *butter wouldn't melt in his* (or *her*) *mouth* is often used of a child who looks very innocent and incapable of doing anything wrong but who in reality is full of mischief. The expression, first recorded in the 16th century, may have arisen because such supposedly virtuous people are thought to be so completely cold and unfeeling that not even a piece of soft butter would melt in their mouths.

butterfly

A *butterfly* is a flying insect with large brightly coloured wings and a thin body. The word is popularly thought to have been formed as a reference to the insect *fluttering by*. The insect does indeed flutter by, but the origin is simpler. The insect, according to its origin, is a *butter-fly*. There are different theories why it was originally known in this way. It may be from the yellow colour of the wings of many kinds of butterfly. Alternatively, according to popular folklore, mischievous witches in the form of butterflies stole butter and milk at night.

buttonhole

If you *buttonhole* someone, you make him or her listen to what you are saying. The origin of this word is not, as might be assumed, the holes through which buttons pass. Rather, *buttonhole* is an alteration of the obsolete verb *buttonhold*, to stop someone from going away by holding the buttons on his or her clothes. This action was undertaken originally in order to sell goods to that person; at a later date, it came to mean detaining someone in conversation.

buxom

Buxom is an example of a word that has changed its meaning in the course of time. In the 12th century, the Old English word for *buxom* (*būhsum*) meant obedient. Coming from the Old English *būgan*, to bend, it was used of both men and women. Towards the end of the 16th century, several meanings developed: 'yielding; obliging', and 'easy-going; lively', all these meanings eventually dying out, and finally 'plump and attractive'. This is the only current sense and applies only to women.

by and large

By and large, meaning in general, has its origin in the days of sailing-ships. The expressions *by the wind* and *sailing large* mean that the wind is before and just behind the beam respectively. So *by and large* implies a balance between two extreme positions or a consideration of things in a broad or general way.

by-law

The *by* in the word *by-law* means local, so a by-law is a law that has application only in a particular area. *By-law* comes from Old Norse *bӯlög*, a town law, from *bӯr*, a town and *lög*, a law. The '-by' is used as an ending of the names of places that were once Scandinavian settlements, e.g. *Grimsby* and *Whitby*.

C

cabal

A *cabal* is a clique, a small group of people who meet secretly or unofficially, especially for the purpose of political intrigue. The word derives ultimately from Hebrew *quabbālāh* 'what is received; tradition'. It is popularly believed, however, that *cabal* originated with the initials of the names of King Charles II's ministers from 1667 to 1673: Sir Thomas *C*lifford (1630–73), Lord *A*shley (later 1st Earl of Shaftesbury) (1621–83), the 2nd Duke of *B*uckingham (1628–87), the 1st Earl of *A*rlington (1618–85), and the Duke of *L*auderdale (1616–82). This powerful political group's scheming and intriguing met with great unpopularity. It was noticed that the ministers' initials made up the word *cabal* and it seems certain that the existence of this faction made the use of the word more current, adding to it pejorative connotations of reproach.

cake (*take the cake*)

To *take the cake* (or *biscuit*) means to be extremely foolish or outrageous; *For rudeness, your brother really takes the cake*! This meaning has developed from the original sense of deserve or win a prize, from a former entertainment among Blacks in Southern US plantations. The idea of the contest was to see who were the most graceful pair of walkers. Participants would walk with fancy steps in a circle round a cake. The cake was the prize — so the winners would quite literally *take the cake*. From these competitions developed the *cakewalk* dance.

calculate

In ancient Roman times, the arithmetical machine was the abacus — a board with slots in which pebbles were moved backwards and forwards to perform the reckoning. From the Latin word for a pebble, *calculus*, comes our word *calculate*. Interestingly, the Latin word *calculus* itself survives in English both as a medical term, in the original sense of stone (e.g. *a renal calculus*, a hard stony mass that forms in the kidney), and as the name of the branch of mathematics that is concerned with variable quantities. See also ABACUS.

candidate

A *candidate* is someone who is seeking or is nominated for a particular position, e.g. for a job or in an election. The word comes from Latin *candidus*, white — in Roman times a candidate for public office would wear a white toga to symbolize his unsullied character and motives. From the word *candidus* developed the meanings 'honest' and 'frank' — senses of our modern word *candid*.

candle (not hold a candle to something)

If someone or something *can't hold a candle* to another person or thing, it isn't good enough to be compared with it: *If it's a matter of efficiency, they can't hold a candle to their overseas competitors*. The expression derives from the days before electricity when candles provided the source of lighting. If a master required light, he employed an apprentice to hold a candle. And someone going home from an inn or theatre would be shown along the dark streets by a boy carrying a torch. Such a task was menial, and those that proved unable to perform this work – those who were not fit to hold the candle – were clearly unfit to do anything. The phrase then came to be used to refer to a person or thing that could only be unfavourably compared with another.

canter

Canter, a horse's gait that is faster than a trot but slower than a gallop – derives from the name of the city of *Canterbury*, England. The word was coined, so tradition has it, to describe the steady pace at which pilgrims rode on horseback to the tomb of Thomas à Becket in Canterbury cathedral.

cardigan

The *cardigan*, the knitted jacket fastened up the front with buttons, or a zip, is named after the British cavalry officer James Thomas Brudenell, 7th Earl of *Cardigan* (1797–1868). The garment was first worn by British soldiers in the extreme cold of the Crimean winter. It was the Earl of Cardigan who led the Charge of the Light Brigade in the most famous battle of the Crimean War, near the village of Balaclava on 25 October 1854. The word for the woollen hood that covers the ears, neck, and throat takes its name from this village. No *balaclava* was in fact worn in the battle and it is thought to have been invented some years later. It was named after the village because of the intense cold endured by the army in the Crimean winter.

carpetbagger

A *carpetbagger* in American English was originally an unscrupulous Northern politician who travelled through the South after the American Civil War, seeking to win political power, business gains, etc., during the period of Reconstruction. They were known as carpetbaggers since they carried all their belongings in travelling-bags made of pieces of carpet sewn together. Nowadays a *carpetbagger* is someone who tries to become a politician in a locality that is not his or her home, especially in the hope of making personal gain.

carry coals to Newcastle

To *carry coals to Newcastle* means to take something to a place where it is already in abundant supply. The phrase refers to *Newcastle-upon-Tyne*, in north-east England, traditionally noted for its coal production. This expression has interesting foreign-language parallels. In French, it is *porter de l'eau à la rivière* (to carry water to the river) and in German *Eulen nach Athen tragen* (to carry owls to Athens).

cast pearls before swine

To *cast pearls before swine* is to offer something valuable to someone who is not able to appreciate it. The phrase goes back to early writings such as the 14th-century William Langland's *Piers Plowman*, 'Noli mittere Margeri – perles Among hogges'. The expression has gained currency from the Authorized (King James) Version of the Bible, Matthew 7:6, 'Give not that which is holy unto the dogs, neither cast ye your pearls before swine, lest they trample them under their feet, and turn again and rend you.'

cat (a cat has nine lives; let the cat out of the bag)

The saying *a cat has nine lives* is a proverb that goes back to at least the 16th century. Cats are considered determined creatures because of their astute, cautious nature; they are known for being able to land safely on their feet after falling from a great height. But why nine lives? One suggestion is the 'holy' number three multiplied by itself.

If you *let the cat out of the bag*, you tell a secret. The origin of the phrase is probably to be found in English country fairs of years gone by. Traders would try to trick unwary customers by putting a cat in a bag, claiming to prospective buyers that it was a suckling pig. Purchasers would then pay without closely examining what they had bought – only later to *let the cat out of the bag* and discover that they had been tricked. See also *a pig in a poke* under PIG.

cat-o'-nine-tails

A *cat-o'-nine-tails* is a rope whip made of nine knotted lines or cords fastened to a handle. Formerly used for flogging criminal offenders, the whip takes its name from the resemblance of the scars that it makes to the scratches of a cat. See also *no room to swing a cat* under ROOM.

catch-22

A *catch-22* or a *catch-22 situation* is a ridiculous dilemma from which someone cannot escape because the means of escape is itself forbidden by the dilemma. The phrase comes from the title of the novel *Catch-22* by the US novelist Joseph Heller (1923–), published in 1961. In the book, American pilots, forced to fly an excessive number of missions, could not be relieved of this duty unless they were diagnosed as insane. On the other hand, pilots who refused to fly (in the hope of being sent home) were obviously not mad, because they were thinking too clearly. In such a *catch-22 situation*, it is impossible to do anything: the mutually exclusive conditions lead to deadlock.

catch someone red-handed

If you *catch someone red-handed*, you catch him or her in the act of committing wrong. The phrase alludes to the discovery of a murderer so soon after committing the crime that the victim's blood is still on the murderer's hands.

caviare to the general

Caviare to the general is something that is considered too delicate to appeal to the appreciation or understanding of the masses. The word *general* in the phrase refers to the general public, not to the military rank. The expression derives from Shakespeare's *Hamlet* (Act 2, Scene ii): 'The play, I remember, pleased not the million; 'twas caviare to the general.' Hamlet is arguing that the play, like caviare, is for discriminating people; others would not appreciate it because they have not acquired a refined taste.

chance one's arm

To *chance one's arm* is to take a risk in order to gain an advantage: *I'm going to chance my arm and hope I won't be caught.* The phrase may have a military origin, referring to the fact that the badges or stripes of military rank are worn on the arm of a uniform. A soldier who was taking a risk that involved the breaking of regulations was *chancing* – risking – *his arm*.

chauvinism

The word *chauvinism*, referring to an excessive unthinking devotion to one's country, comes from the name of the French soldier Nicolas *Chauvin* of Rochefort. A soldier in Napoleon's army and wounded many times, Chauvin was ridiculed by his fellow-soldiers for his fanatical devotion to Napoleon. Even when Chauvin was pensioned off with a medal, a ceremonial sabre, and a meagre pension of 200 francs a year, his patriotic zeal continued unabated.

The dramatists Charles and Jean Cogniard made the name *Chauvin* famous in their comedy *Le Cocarde Tricolore* (1831). In this, Chauvin is a young recruit who sings several songs with the chorus that includes the lines, '*Je suis français, je suis Chauvin*'. The character of Chauvin later featured in a number of other French comedies and as a result became widely known. The word *chauvinism* soon became familiar in English to describe fanatical patriotism. In more recent years, the sense of the word has widened to include an unreasoned and prejudiced belief in the superiority of one's group or cause, e.g. in the expression *male chauvinism*.

cheat

In feudal times, an *escheator* looked after lands that reverted to a feudal lord when there were no legal heirs to the property. The escheators also had the task of collecting rents and taxes. They had the reputation of being unscrupulous and so came to be known as cheaters – and hence our verb *cheat*, to act dishonestly or lie for one's own benefit.

cheek (turn the other cheek)

To *turn the other cheek* means to respond to unkindness or harm with patience; not to retaliate when one is provoked, but even to be prepared to accept further unkindness, etc. The expression is derived from the words of Jesus, recorded in the Authorized (King James) Version of the Bible, Matthew 5:39: 'But I say unto you, That ye resist not evil: but whosoever shall smite thee on thy right cheek, turn to him the other also'.

cherry

The small round soft fruit known as a *cherry* takes its name from the Old Northern French *cherise*, incorrectly thought of as a plural, from Latin *cerasum*, of *Cerasus*. Cerasus, now Giresun, in north-east Turkey, was the place from which the gourmet Lucullus (?110–56BC), it is said, introduced the cherry into Italy.

chess

The game of *chess* is derived from an Indian game that dates from before the 6th century AD. The game passed via Persia to the Arabs, reaching Europe in about the 10th century. The English name of the game comes via French from the Persian word *shāh*, a king or ruler. So the game may quite legitimately be called the game of kings.

Checkmate, the winning position in which an opponent's king is under attack and escape is impossible, derives ultimately from Persian *shāh māt*, the king is helpless. By the 14th century, the word *checkmate* had come into figurative use to mean to frustrate or defeat.

one's chickens come home to roost

The saying that one's *chickens come home to roost* means that the wrongs done to others will return to the one who originated them – just as chickens return to their roost for the night. The proverb dates back at least to 1810 in the form 'Curses are like young chickens; they always come home to roost', found in the poem *The Curse of Kehama* by the English poet Robert Southey (1774–1843).

the Chiltern Hundreds

The *Chiltern Hundreds* are a nominal office for which a British Member of Parliament applies as a means of resigning his or her seat. The *Chiltern Hundreds* were part of the *Chiltern* hills in Buckinghamshire, England, a *hundred* being a historical subdivision of a county. Years ago the Chilterns were troubled by many bands of robbers and stewards were appointed to restore order. In the course of time, the need for such stewards disappeared. The office survives, however, although now a wholly honorary one and is used in the resigning of an MP. An MP may not simply resign, so when wishing to do so, he or she applies for (*Stewardship of*) *the Chiltern Hundreds*, and holding this office of profit under the crown disqualifies him or her from being an MP.

chip (*have a chip on one's shoulder*)

To *have a chip on one's shoulder* means to behave in an aggressive or rude way because one feels inferior or because one considers that one has been unfairly treated. The phrase was known from at least the early 19th century in the USA. A boy would put a chip of wood on his shoulder and dare anyone to knock it off and fight him, so someone who *has a chip on his or her shoulder* is spoiling for trouble.

chivvy

To *chivvy* or *chivy* someone is to urge him or her constantly to do something, to harass. The word *chivvy* was a hunting cry, the word deriving probably from the *Cheviot* Hills on the border between England and Scotland and the scene of many border battles. One such battle, the Battle of Otterburn (1388) was described in *the Ballad of Chevy Chase*, in which the neighbouring families of Percy (England) and Douglas (Scotland) fought. Percy vowed to hunt for three days across the Scottish border without the Scots' agreement. The result was that the two sides met and fought, great slaughter ensued, and both leaders were killed. The ballad relates the story of this battle, and it seems probable that the word *chivvy* comes from the title of the ballad.

chop suey

Chop suey is the Chinese-style dish of chopped meat or chicken, beansprouts and other vegetables such as mushrooms cooked in a sauce and served with rice. The meal does not originate in China, as might be supposed, but was invented in America in the late-19th century. The name of the dish has nothing to do with the English word *chop*, but comes from Chinese (Cantonese) *shap sui*, odds and ends. It seems that the chef who first devised the dish took various leftover pieces of meat and vegetables to produce this Chinese-style meal.

chortle

To *chortle* means to laugh with satisfaction or amusement. The word was coined by Lewis Carroll in *Through the Looking Glass* (1872) by joining the words *chuckle* and *snort*. Another word that he coined which has passed into general use is *squawk*, from *squeal* and *squall*. Carroll called such words portmanteau words (a portmanteau being a then fashionable kind of suitcase), since the two meanings were 'packed' into one word.

claptrap

If you say that something is *claptrap*, you mean that it is foolish nonsense. A *claptrap* comes from the language of the theatre and was originally a means of trapping (hand) claps. In other words, it referred to a playwright's trick of catching applause from an audience. Because such a trick was not in any way connected with the show itself, the word *claptrap* later came to be used generally to refer to irrelevant and worthless talk.

clean (as clean as a whistle; make a clean breast of something)

If something is *as clean as a whistle*, it is completely clean and free from any dirt, etc.; or, figuratively, perfectly neat or accurate. The *whistle* referred to in this simile is one made of wood, usually a reed. So in order to produce a clear sound, the whistle had to be perfectly clean – free from dust, dirt, and other impurities.

To *make a clean breast of something* means to confess it fully. The phrase goes back to the ancient religious tradition of marking a sinner's breast with ashes to symbolize the sins that he or she had committed. So to make a clean breast of something was to admit and confess one's sins and so be purified.

cloud-cuckoo-land

If you say that someone is living in *cloud-cuckoo-land*, he or she is living in an imaginary world that is idealistic and impractical and bears little resemblance to reality. The expression is a translation of a Greek phrase in the comedy *The Birds* by the Athenian dramatist Aristophanes (?448–?380BC). In this play, the birds built an imaginary city in the air, a kind of cloud-cuckoo-land.

clue

A *clue* is something that provides guidance on how to solve a problem. The word is a variant of *clew*, a ball of thread. In particular, the word was used to show one's way out of a labyrinth. The history of the word goes back to the story of the Greek hero Theseus and the Minotaur, the monster that was half-human and half-bull, who lived in the Labyrinth, the maze built for King Minos on Crete. Ariadne, the king's daughter, gave Theseus a sword to kill the monster and also a ball of thread. Theseus unravelled the thread as he entered the labyrinth and, after killing the monster, wound it up again as he came out. So a *clue* is something that suggests a way of solving a puzzle.

coach

A *coach* nowadays is a (usually single-decked) bus for long-distance travel or a railway carriage that forms part of a train. The word derives from the Hungarian *kocsi szekér*, a wagon from *Kocs*, a village in north-west Hungary where the first horse-drawn coaches were made in the 15th century. The word passed into German as *Kutsche* and was taken into French as *coche*, the form from which our English word comes.

The use of *coach*, in the sense of an instructor, probably comes from the idea that a tutor 'carries' a student through a course and an examination.

the coast is clear

The expression *the coast is clear* means that a particular source of danger or interference has now passed and an action may be proceeded with. The phrase was originally used by smugglers in its literal sense — that the coast was clear of coastguards, and so it was safe to carry on the secret operations.

cobalt

The word *cobalt*, the hard whitish metallic element that is used widely in alloys, comes ultimately from Middle High German *kobolt*, goblin. This raises the quite legitimate question, 'What is the connection between cobalt and goblins?' Cobalt occurs in silver ore. One suggestion is that the deposits of cobalt in silver ore were thought to be due to the work of goblins. Or according to an alternative theory, the poor health of the cobalt miners was ascribed to the malice of the goblins that were thought to live in the mines.

a cobbler should stick to his last

The expression *a cobbler should stick to his last* means that one should not interfere in matters that are beyond one's area of knowledge. The saying derives from a story of Apelles, the 4th-century BC Greek artist and the favourite painter of Alexander the Great. A cobbler criticized the drawing of a fastening on a sandal in one of Apelles' pictures. Apelles rectified the error. But when the cobbler had the nerve to criticize his drawing of the legs, Apelles (in the words of Pliny) is said to have replied, '*Ne supra crepidam sutor judicaret*' (The cobbler should not judge above his last), a *last* being the foot-shaped form on which a cobbler makes and repairs shoes. In other words, the cobbler should keep to his trade of shoe-making and not meddle in professions that he knows little or nothing about.

cock-and-bull story

A *cock-and-bull story* is a long, improbable tale. The origin of this phrase may well go back to Aesop's fables – stories in which animals spoke to one another using human language. Since conversations were clearly in reality impossible, any unbelievable tale, for example one offered as an excuse, came to be thought of as a *cock-and-bull story*. The expression occurs at the end of the novel *Tristram Shandy* (1759–67) by Laurence Sterne, 'What is all this story about? – A Cock and a Bull, said Yorick – And one of the best of its kind, I ever heard.' This occurrence has helped to establish the phrase in the language.

coconut

The word for a *coconut*, the large oval fruit that has a hard hairy shell and contains a milky juice and white edible lining, has its origins in the Portuguese word *côco*, bogeyman. The Portuguese who gave the coconut this name saw in the base of the nut, with its three dark holes, a resemblance to a gruesome grinning face.

cold (give someone/get the cold shoulder)

If you *give someone the cold shoulder* (or someone *gets the cold shoulder*), you snub someone – you behave in an unfriendly way towards him or her. The expression is said to derive from the dish of a *cold shoulder* of mutton served to a guest who had outstayed a welcome or to an ordinary traveller whose presence was not warmly received. Such an unexceptional meal stood in comparison to the delicious hot meal served to a welcome guest or important visitor. The compound verb *cold-shoulder* has the same meaning as *give the cold shoulder*.

companion

A *companion* is someone who accompanies a person. The word derives ultimately from Latin *cum*, with or together, and *panis*, bread, so a companion was originally someone with whom one ate bread. From this came the sense of a friend or someone travelling with a person.

complexion

A person's *complexion* is the colouring and appearance of the skin on his or her face. The word derives from the medieval idea that a person's temperament was determined by the precise proportions in which four fluids were combined in the body. The four liquids or *humours* were bile (choler), black bile (melancholy), blood, and phlegm. For example, if a man was ruddy, it was thought that blood was the main 'humour' or fluid in his system, and his complexion was regarded as sanguine. The combination of the fluids was regarded as all-important in determining a person's temperament, hence the adoption of Latin *complexio*, from *complectere*, to plait or braid together. Since the colour of a person's face was thought to give an important clue to his or her complexion or disposition, the sense of *complexion* 'the combination of the four humours of the body', gradually became 'the colouring and appearance of the facial skin'.

a conspiracy of silence

A *conspiracy of silence* is an agreement by people not to talk about something, for example to further one's own selfish purposes. The expression is said to have been coined by the Welsh poet Sir Lewis Morris (1833–1907). Feeling that his achievements were being neglected, he is reputed to have complained to Oscar Wilde that no one reviewed his work, saying, 'Oscar, there's a conspiracy of silence against me. What shall I do?' Wilde answered, 'Join it!'

constable

A *constable* in British English is a policeman or policewoman of the lowest rank. The status designated by this word has been higher, however, in earlier times. The word derives from Late Latin *comes stabuli*, an officer or attendant of the stable. In the course of time those having this rank were entrusted with greater responsibilities and when *constable* entered the English language in the 13th century it had come to stand for 'Master of the Horse', the high-ranking chief officer of royal or noble households. The association of *constable* with law enforcement and maintaining the peace came in the 14th century. See also MARSHAL.

cook someone's goose

To *cook someone's goose* means to spoil someone's chance of success. The expression was traditionally thought to go back to an old story about the citizens of a besieged town in medieval times. The townspeople were so contemptuous of their attackers that they hung a goose from a tower – the goose symbolizing stupidity. Unfortunately their plan went wrong and the attackers were so angry at this taunt that they burnt the whole town down – literally *cooking the goose* as well. This story, though interesting, does not stand up to academic research, since the phrase first appeared in English, it seems, about 1850.

cordial

Cordial behaviour is friendly and warm: *a cordial invitation to our reception*. According to the history of the word *cordial*, all feelings described in this way should be heartfelt, since the word derives from Latin *cor*, a heart. This origin also explains the reason that *cordial* was formerly used to describe a medicine or drink that was supposed to stimulate the heart.

The meaning 'a sweet non-alcoholic fruit drink' (*a lime cordial*) derives from this usage.

cordon bleu

Cordon bleu is used to describe cookery of the finest quality. *Cordon bleu* is French for 'blue-ribbon', the blue ribbon having for a long time been the sign of the highest standard in a particular field, for example to refer to the ship that crosses the Atlantic Ocean the fastest. The highest order of British knighthood is the Order of the Garter, founded by King Edward III in 1348. The order's badge is a dark blue velvet silk ribbon worn on the left leg below the knee. Inscribed on the garter is the motto, *Honi soit qui mal y pense* ('The shame be his who thinks evil of it'). These are popularly believed to have been the words of Edward III when he tied to his own leg a garter dropped by a lady at a party, in order to save her from embarrassment. In France, the *cordon bleu* was originally the blue ribbon of the knight's grand cross of the Order of the Holy Spirit, the first order of the Bourbon kings, and it later came to be used to honour the finest chefs.

corduroy

There are at least three explanations of the word *corduroy*, a thick cotton cloth with a ribbed pattern. The most popular theory nowadays is that the word derives from *cord*, a ribbed fabric, and *duroy*, an obsolete term for a coarse West of England woollen material. The possibility that the word comes from French *corde du roi*, a cord of the king – said to have referred to a fabric woven from silk and used by French kings when hunting – is unlikely, as no such word has been used by the French. A third suggestion is that the word derives from the surname *Corderoy*, its manufacturer or designer.

corny

Something that is *corny* is hackneyed or very simple and sentimental. The word is a shortening of *corn-fed*, which was used to describe the supposedly unsophisticated audiences of farmers, for example in the *Corn Belt* of the Mid-West USA. These audiences were said to delight so much in humour that was not at all subtle, that the humour became known as *corn-fed humour*, which later became *corny* jokes.

the corridors of power

The phrase *the corridors of power* is used to describe the places in government and administration where important decisions are made. In such influential places, people jockey for position. The phrase was coined by the English writer, scientist, and administrator C.P. Snow (1905–80) and was used as the title of his novel, published in 1963, describing Westminster life.

countdown

A *countdown*, the calling out of numbers in reverse order to zero, did not originate with the launching of space rockets at Cape Canaverel, as is generally thought. The originator of the *countdown* technique was in fact the Austrian-born American film director Fritz Lang (1890–1976), known especially for his direction of the silent film thriller *M* (1931). Lang devised the *countdown* technique for the rocket launching in his science-fiction film *Die Frau im Mond* (*The Lady in the Moon*) (1928).

coup de grâce

A *coup de grâce* is a decisive action or event that finally destroys something. It may come as a surprise therefore to know that the expression, literally translated, means 'a stroke of mercy'. In former times, a condemned prisoner was tortured on a rack or wheel for long periods, before being finally given a *coup de grâce* – a blow that would kill him – a 'stroke of mercy' that would remove his agony.

cover a multitude of sins

If something *covers a multitude of sins*, it deliberately hides many different things, especially faults and weaknesses. The expression comes from the Authorized (King James) Version of the Bible, 1 Peter 4:8: 'And above all things have fervent charity among yourselves: for charity shall cover the multitude of sins.'

coward

A *coward* is someone who lacks courage and avoids dangerous or difficult situations. The word derives ultimately from Latin *cauda*, a tail. The allusion is probably to a frightened animal cowering with its tail between its legs.

cowslip

A *cowslip* is a small plant of the primrose family with fragrant yellow flowers. The plant does not derive its name from its similarity with a cow's lip, as might be supposed. In fact, *cowslip* means 'cow dung' (from Old English *cū*, cow, and *slyppe* or *slypa*, paste), the flower being frequently found in pastures where cows grazed. Modern English *slip*, the semi-liquid mixture of water and fine clay used in pottery, derives from this same old English word.

cravat

A *cravat* is a neck scarf or necktie that a man wears round his neck tucked inside an open-necked shirt. The word is a 17th-century borrowing of the French *cravate*. The original cravats were scarves worn by Croatian soldiers recruited by the French army during the Thirty Years' War (1618–48). The French adopted this garment as a fashion, calling it a *cravate*, from the French *Cravate*, a Croatian. Croatia is now a republic of northern Yugoslavia.

creosote

Creosote is a thick dark oily liquid that is made from coal tar and is used to preserve wood. The word in the original means 'flesh-preserver', deriving as it does ultimately from Greek, *kreas*, flesh, and *sōtēr*, preserver. This was because the name was originally applied to a different liquid – one with antiseptic qualities. This liquid was produced from wood tar and was used in medical treatment.

cretin

If you call someone a *cretin*, you think that he or she is an idiot. This offensive term has its origins in the French word for a Christian. In medieval times, some physically deformed and mentally retarded people lived in the Swiss Alpine regions. This condition was a result of a thyroid gland deficiency. The Swiss French word used to describe these people was *crestin*, from Latin *Christianus*, Christian, in allusion to their humanity, despite their deformity. The favourable term passed into French as *crétin*, an idiot, and it kept this meaning in English.

criss-cross

The word *criss-cross*, referring to a pattern of intersecting lines, comes from *Christ's cross*, the cross of Christ. This word derives in part from the mark of a cross in a children's 16th-century hornbook primer, which was a sheet of paper mounted on a wooden tablet and protected by a thin plate of horn. The paper listed the alphabet, the Lord's Prayer, and some numbers. The alphabet that was printed on the top line of the paper was preceded by a small Maltese cross known as the *Christ-cross* or *Christ's cross*. The row of letters in the alphabet became known as *Christ-cross row*, this in time becoming changed to *criss-cross*.

The word *criss-cross* is also usually considered to be a reduplication of sounds based on the word *cross*, with the vowel changing (other examples of reduplication being *dilly-dally* and *ding-dong*).

crocodile tears

Someone who sheds *crocodile tears* pretends to be very sad or sorry. The phrase comes from an old folk story. According to the story, the sly crocodile wept copiously, uttering loud sighs and moans in order to appear upset and so lure curious passers-by. When the victims came within reach, they would then immediately be taken hold of and devoured. So *crocodile tears* came to stand for feigned sorrow.

cross the Rubicon

To *cross the Rubicon* means to commit oneself irrevocably to a particular course of action. The expression derives from the river *Rubicon* in North Italy that in ancient Roman times formed part of the boundary between Cisalpine Gaul and Italy. In 49 BC Julius Caesar, then provincial commander in Gaul, led his army across the Rubicon into Italy to march on

Rome. Such an action was in effect a declaration of civil war, since a general was not permitted to lead an army outside the province to which he had been sent. So by *crossing the Rubicon*, Caesar was an invader and was committing himself irrevocably to civil war. Or in the words attributed to Caesar, 'Jacta alea est,' (The die is cast): there was no going back. See also *the die is cast* under DIE.

cry wolf

To *cry wolf* is to give a false alarm of danger. The phrase derives from the fable of a shepherd boy who as a hoax shouted, 'wolf!', in an attempt to make the villagers come to protect the sheep from attacks by the supposed wolves. The boy did this so often that when one day a wolf really did come and attack his sheep and he cried out, no one believed him and so all his sheep were killed.

cupboard love

Cupboard love is insincere affection shown with the selfish or greedy intention of gaining something for oneself. The allusion is to the show of love by children to their parents who will satisfy their children's wishes by giving them some tasty food from the store cupboard.

curate (like the curate's egg)

The expression *like the curate's egg*, referring to something that has both good and bad parts, derives from a cartoon in *Punch* (9 November 1895). The cartoon shows a nervous curate who, while eating breakfast with his bishop, is served with a bad egg. The bishop remarks, 'I'm afraid your egg is bad,' to which the curate, not wanting to offend his host, replies, 'Oh no, my lord, I assure you! Parts of it are excellent.'

curfew

A *curfew* is an order that states that people should stay in their homes after a particular time at night until the next morning. The word derives from Middle French *covrefeu*, a signal to cover the fire. In medieval times there was a great danger of a fire spreading through a town at night, so a bell was sounded at a certain hour to warn all the townspeople to extinguish their fires. The French word passed into English as *curfew* and this word later came to be used for the regulation – used particularly in times of civil unrest – that requires people to withdraw from the streets by the time that is specified.

curry favour

The expression *curry favour*, meaning to try to gain favour by flattery or attention, has nothing to do with the spicy oriental dish. The phrase is an alteration of the Middle English expression *curry favel*. To *curry* means to groom or stroke down a horse; *Favel* (or *Fauvel*) was the name of a chestnut horse in a 14th-century French satirical poem, the *Roman de Favel*. Favel symbolized cunning or hypocrisy, so to *curry favel* was to try to ingratiate oneself through insincere means. Later, *favel* became *favour*, because of the association of sound and meaning with that word.

cut the Gordian knot

To *cut the Gordian knot* is to solve a complex problem by a single decisive, brilliant action. The expression alludes to the story of *Gordius*, the peasant King of Phrygia in Asia Minor. Gordius dedicated his chariot to Jupiter, fastening the yoke to the beam of his chariot with such an intricate knot that no one could untie it. The legend developed that whoever could untie the knot would reign over the whole of Asia. When Alexander the Great passed through the town (333 BC) he is said to have simply cut the knot with his sword and so claimed fulfilment of the legend in himself.

cut of one's jib

If you assess people by the *cut of their jib*, your judgment rests on their overall appearance or general way in which they do things. The expression dates back to the age of sailing-ships, when a captain would seek to recognize an approaching ship by its jib – the triangular sail set forward of a vessel's foremast. Each nationality had its own characteristic and identifiable way of cutting its jib sail. So if the captain didn't like the *cut of the jib* of an advancing vessel, he would be suspicious and steer clear of it.

cut someone to the quick

The *quick* in this expression is a highly sensitive area of flesh, especially that under the finger-nails or toe-nails. The word derives from Old English *cwicu*, living. So to *cut someone to the quick* means literally to cut through the skin to the painfully sensitive living tissue, and figuratively, to hurt or upset someone very deeply: *His callous remarks really cut me to the quick.* Other examples of *quick* in the sense of 'living' include the phrase *the quick and the dead* of the Authorized (King James) Version of the Bible.

cynic

A *cynic* is someone who doubts people's sincerity and often shows this with sarcasm. The term derives from the followers of the Greek philosopher Antisthenes (c.445–c.360 BC), especially his later disciples such as Diogenes (411–322 BC), who were known as *Cynics*. There are two theories of the origin of this word. One is that the members of the sect were rude and churlish in manner, hence Greek *kynikos*, dog-like. The other theory is that the sect met in a school called *Kynosarges*, Greek for white dog, as it was supposed that a white dog had once carried off part of a sacrifice being offered to the gods.

Whatever the precise origin of their name, the Cynics were scornful of the accepted values of the rest of society. They tended to live unconventional lives, believing in the self-sufficiency of the individual and that virtue was the highest good, the way to goodness being through self-control. It was, however, the negative aspects of the Cynics' beliefs that came to be emphasized, leading to the contemporary sense of the word, someone who believes that people are motivated by selfishness.

D

D-day

What does the *D* in *D-day* stand for? It simply stands for *day*. The term was used in World War II to refer to the day (6 June 1944) on which the invasion of France was begun by the forces allied against Germany. In fact the term had already been used in World War I to refer to the day of the allied forces' offensive at St Mihiel (between Verdun and Nancy) on 17 September 1918. Nowadays the expression is used to refer to the day that is chosen for the beginning of an important activity. *H*(our)-*hour* is used similarly, to mark the exact time of day of the launch of an operation.

daffodil

The plant with a large yellow trumpet-shaped flower known as a *daffodil* (botanically a plant of the Narcissus genus) comes ultimately from the Greek *asphodelos*, the flower which according to Greek legend covered the Elysian fields. It seems that in the 15th century, the word *asphodel* began to be called *affodill*, and was applied by mistake to a species of narcissus. Later the *d* was added to give *daffodil*, possibly because of a further mistake, a joining of the two Dutch words *de affodil*, the asphodel.

daisy

The *daisy*, the common European plant with usually white petal-like rays round a centre, derives from Old English *dægesēage*, day's eye, from *dæg*, day, and *ēage*, eye. The flower is so called because of its appearance and because it closes its rays in the evening to hide its yellow centre and opens them again in the morning.

damask

Damask is a kind of firm cloth, for example linen, cotton or silk, with a pattern woven into it, that is used for tablecloths, curtains, etc. The name goes back to the 14th century and comes from *Damascus*, Syria, where this silk fabric was originally made. The patterns were imitated by weavers in France and Flanders and later brought into England.

Damascus was also known for its workers in fine metal. *Damascus steel* was a hard flexible steel developed in medieval times. The steel was made by forging metal in strips, to give a wavy pattern on its surface and was used for the blades of swords. Hence the verb *damascene*, to decorate a metal with such a wavy pattern or with an inlay of precious metals.

The *damask rose*, a large fragrant pink rose, was originally 'rose of Damascus'.

damn with faint praise

To *damn with faint praise* is to imply criticism or disapproval by praising qualities that have only a slight importance. The phrase derives from the *Epistle to Dr Arbuthnot* (1735) by the English poet Alexander Pope (1688–1744), in which Pope satirizes the essayist and man of letters Joseph Addison:

Damn with faint praise, assent with civil leer,
And, without sneering, teach the rest to sneer.

dandelion

The *dandelion*, a kind of common weed with bright-yellow flowers, was in the 16th century originally Middle French *dent de lion*, lion's tooth – so called because of the shape of its leaves. *Dent de lion* gradually became changed to the present form, *dandelion*. In other languages the resemblance to the lion's tooth is also alluded to, e.g. German *Löwenzahn*, Spanish *diente de león*.

a Daniel come to judgment

The expression *a Daniel come to judgment* is used to refer to a person of upright character who makes a wise decision about a matter that has puzzled others. The phrase alludes to the story of Daniel in the apocryphal History of Susanna in which Daniel's wisdom and skill saved Susanna from a false accusation of adultery. The phrase itself originates in Shakespeare's *The Merchant of Venice* (Act 4, Scene i):

> A Daniel come to judgement! yea a Daniel!
> O wise young judge, how I do honour thee!

a dark horse

A *dark horse* is someone who does not make his or her abilities, intentions, etc., widely known. The phrase comes from horse racing: a dark horse was a comparatively unknown horse, whose abilities were kept secret until it came on to the track ... and unexpectedly showed its skill by winning the race. The first literary usage is attributed to the novel *The Young Duke* (1831) by Benjamin Disraeli: 'A dark horse, which had never been thought of, and which the careless St James had never even observed in the list, rushed past the grandstand in sweeping triumph.'

The first political dark horse is generally regarded as James K. Polk – a relatively unknown candidate introduced to break the deadlock at the Democratic convention of 1844. Polk went on to become president (1845–49).

Davy Jones' locker

The bottom of the sea, thought of as the grave of those drowned or buried at sea, is known as *Davy Jones' locker*. Davy Jones is seen as a personification of the devil who rules over the evil spirits of the sea. Being part of sailor slang for over 200 years, there are several different theories of how the expression originated.

Some suggest that *Jones* is an alteration of the name of the biblical *Jonah*, thrown overboard from a ship and swallowed by a great fish. The name *Davy* is said to have been added by Welsh sailors, *David* being the patron saint of Wales.

Other sources say that Davy is an anglicization of the West Indian word *duffy* or *duppy*, malevolent ghost.

Still others hold the *Davy Jones* was originally the owner of a 16th-century London public house that was popular with sailors. The pub is said to have also served as a place for press-ganging unwary seamen into service: Davy Jones was thought to store more than just ale in the lockers at the back of the pub. The sailors would be drugged, transferred to a ship, to awaken only when the ship had put to sea. Thus Davy Jones' locker came to be feared.

dead (as dead as the dodo; as dead as a doornail; a dead ringer)

If something is described as being *as dead as the* (or *a*) *dodo*, it is completely out of date or no longer in existence. The simile alludes to the extinct species of flightless bird that once inhabited Mauritius. The birds were larger and heavier than swans and were probably extinct by the 18th century.

Someone or something that is *as dead as a doornail* is completely dead, or, figuratively, no longer has any importance. The phrase was first used in the 14th-century *Vision of Piers Plowman*, but what does the expression mean? It may be that the doornail was the metal plate against which a door knocker banged. As this was hit so many times over the years, it could understandably have had all its life struck from it, and so be dead. An alternative suggestion is that the doornail was the large-headed nail formerly used to provide a fastening for a door by turning over the nail's point. This clinching of the nail made the joint secure and the nail 'dead' – not easily removable.

If a person is a *dead ringer* for someone else, he or she looks exactly like that other person. The *ringer* here was originally in US usage a superior horse that is fraudulently substituted for another one (an unknown) in a race. The *dead* means 'exact' or 'absolute', as in *dead heat*, *dead centre*, etc.

deadline

A *deadline* is a time by which a certain task or job has to be finished: *We'll all have to work harder to meet next Tuesday's deadline*. The original deadline was a line or boundary marked out round a fence at a prisoner-of-war camp in the American Civil War. Any prisoner who tried to cross the line risked being shot by a guard.

death (at death's door)

If someone is *at death's door*, he or she is extremely ill and at the point of dying. The expression comes from the translation by Miles Coverdale of Psalm 107:18 in the Book of Common Prayer: 'Their soul abhorred all manner of meat: and they were even hard at death's door.'

debt

Debt, something owed, comes from Old French *dette*. The *b* was inserted by scholars in the Middle Ages who assumed that the word derived from Latin *debitum*. At about this time printing was introduced and so the spelling of words became fixed. Hence the *b* of *debt* has remained with us ever since. Similar insertions are the extra *b* in *doubt* (Middle English *doute*, Latin *dubitare*) and the *p* in *receipt* (Middle English *receite*, Latin *recepta*).

decibel

The *decibel* is the unit that is used to compare two power levels, especially of the intensity of sound, on a logarithmic scale. The decibel is one-tenth of a *bel*, although the latter unit is only rarely used. Both units are named after the Scottish-born US scientist Alexander Graham *Bell* (1847–1922). Bell is famous for his invention of the telephone (1876) – the historic words that Bell spoke to his assistant Thomas Watson on the telephone were, 'Watson, come here, I want you.'

decimate

To *decimate* in general usage means to kill or destroy a large part of: *The famine completely decimated the country's population.* Some speakers and writers of English, however, prefer to restrict the usage of the verb to its original sense of killing or destroying one tenth of – from Latin *decem*, ten. When, in the ancient Roman army, soldiers were guilty of mutiny or cowardice, they were punished by having one in ten of their number chosen by lot and killed.

denim

Denim is the name given to the durable twilled cotton fabric (usually blue) used to make clothes such as trousers or jeans (*denims*). The word was used in Britain from the 17th century for a kind of serge material made in Nîmes, a city in southern France, the name of the fabric originally being *(serge) de Nîmes*.

derrick

A *derrick*, a hoisting apparatus or crane, formerly described a gallows. The word derives from the 17th-century English hangman surnamed *Derrick*. Derrick served under the command of Robert Devereux, 2nd Earl of Essex in the sacking of Cádiz (1596), where he was charged with rape and found guilty. He was sentenced to death by hanging but was pardoned by Essex when he agreed to become executioner at Tyburn gallows, London, near what is now Marble Arch. A few years later, Essex was found guilty of treason after instigating a riot in London (1601) and was sentenced to death, it being Derrick who was to execute him. On this occasion Derrick used an axe, requiring three attempts to cut off Essex's head. In all, Derrick is said to have carried out more than 3000 executions in his service as hangman, his name being applied to the gallows itself and then to the crane that the gallows resembled.

desultory

If something is described as *desultory*, it is unplanned or unmethodical: *merely desultory attempts to support our campaign*. The word originates from ancient Roman circuses, where riders jumped from one horse or chariot to another. Such an acrobat was known as a *desultor*, leaper, from Latin *salire*, to leap. So our word *desultory* came to refer to something that passed from one thing to another fitfully, and hence something that was disconnected or superficial.

deus ex machina

The Latin phrase *deus ex machina* (literally, a god out of a machine) refers to the unexpected intervention of a power or event that resolves an apparently impossible situation, particularly in a contrived or improbable way. The expression derives from theatrical language of ancient Greece and Rome. The ancient playwrights introduced a *deus ex machina* to resolve an intricate plot: an actor playing a god was let down on to the stage by means of a mechanical device in order to decide the final outcome.

devil (between the devil and the deep blue sea, the devil to pay)

If someone is *between the devil and the deep blue sea*, he or she is faced with the choice of two equally unpleasant alternatives. The expression is nautical in origin. The *devil* is not Satan but the seam on the hull of a ship or the heavy plank (the gunwale or gunnel) on a ship's side that was used to support the guns. If a sailor was caught *between the devil and the deep blue sea*, he was in a very precarious position.

The saying *the devil to pay*, trouble is to be expected as a result of some action, derives from the longer expression *there's the devil to pay and no hot pitch*. Here, the devil is the seam on a ship's hull. To *pay* comes from Old French *peier*, to cover with hot pitch. So *the devil to pay and no hot pitch* meant that a task needed to be undertaken but resources for it were not available at the time – so one was obviously in difficulty.

devil (let the devil take the hindmost; devil's advocate)

The saying *let the devil take the hindmost* is a shortening of the expression *each* (or *every*) *man for himself and the devil take the hindmost.* The phrase, meaning look after one's own interests and leave others to look after themselves, first appeared in the play *Philaster* (written about 1610) by Sir Francis Beaumont (1584–1616) and John Fletcher (1579–1625). According to a medieval superstition, would-be disciples of the devil had to train at an establishment in Toledo, Spain. One of the tasks in the 'education' was running along an underground passage. The last one in the race – *the hindmost* – was seized by the devil to become his slave.

A *devil's advocate* is someone who supports an opposing or less popular viewpoint for the sake of argument. The expression derives from Latin *advocatus diaboli*, the name of an official in the Roman Catholic Church who opposes the *advocatus dei* (God's advocate) in discussions on whether a candidate is suitable for canonization or beatification. The technical name for the devil's advocate is *promotor fidei*, Latin for 'promoter of the faith'.

dickens *(what, how etc the dickens)*

The *dickens* in such phrases as *What the dickens do you think you're doing here?* has no connection with the writer Charles Dickens. *Dickens* in this usage is found in Shakespeare (*The Merry Wives of Windsor*, Act 3, Scene ii: 'I cannot tell what the dickens his name is.') It is a euphemism for *devil.*

the die is cast

The expression *the die is cast* means that an important decision has been taken from which there is no turning back. The phrase does not allude to the permanent forming of a metal mould, as is generally supposed, but to the throwing of dice. Once the dice has been thrown, the player has to accept the luck that has been allotted to him or her by the fall of the dice.

The expression *the die is cast* is the translation of Caesar's famous phrase, 'Jacta alea est,' uttered when he crossed the Rubicon. See CROSS THE RUBICON.

diesel

A *diesel* engine is an internal-combustion engine in which fuel is ignited by highly compressed air. The engine is named after the German mechanical engineer Ruldolf *Diesel* (1858–1913), who invented it in 1892. Diesel developed the engine at the Krupp factory in Essen; and he not only invented a new kind of engine, he also found the best kind of fuel, the relatively cheap semi-refined crude oil, to power it. Today the diesel engine is widely used in industry and road, rail, and maritime transport.

dirge

A *dirge* is a slow mournful piece of music or song played or sung for example at a funeral. The word derives from the Latin song, '*Dirige, Domine, Deus meus, in conspectu tuo viam meam*' (Psalm 5:8), 'Guide, O Lord, my God, my way in Thy sight'. Because this line was repeated so often, the service became known by its first word, *dirige*, which in time was changed to *dirge*, the name by which such a funeral song became known.

dismal

Something that is sad, gloomy or of low quality may be described as *dismal*. This modern meaning of the word as an adjective goes back to its use as a noun in the Middle Ages, when it referred to a list of 24 days (2 in each month) that were marked on a calendar as being unlucky. The noun comes from Medieval Latin *dies mali*, evil days, from *dies*, day, and *malus*, bad.

distaff

The *distaff* side is the female side of a family line. The word
goes back to the Middle Ages: a distaff was the staff for holding
the flax or wool in spinning. Since spinning was the work of
the woman, *distaff* came to stand for the domain of women.
The opposite of the distaff side, the male line of descent, is
known as the *spear* side.

do as you would be done by

The moral encouragement *do as you would be done by* means
'treat others in the way that you would like them to treat you'.
The expression originated in a letter from Philip Dormer Stan-
hope, 4th Earl of Chesterfield (1694–1773) to his son: 'Do as
you would be done by is the surest method that I know of
pleasing.' The phrase inspired the creation of the characters
Mrs Doasyouwouldbedoneby and her counterpart Mrs Bedone-
byasyoudid in *The Water-Babies* (1863) by Charles Kingsley
(1819–75).

Dr Livingstone, I presume

The greeting *Doctor Livingstone, I presume* was spoken by Henry
Morton Stanley in 1871 at the conclusion of his search for the
missionary David Livingstone in the heart of Africa. The jour-
nalist Stanley had been sent to Africa by James Gordon
Bennett, the proprietor of the *New York Herald*, to search for
Livingstone, who was thought to be lost. Stanley found him in
Ujiji (now in Tanzania), after a long search. The greeting is
still sometimes used informally or humorously, with a relevant
name substituted, when people meet, especially when such a
meeting is unexpected. The expression is noted for its traditional British meticulous politeness even in the unlikeliest situation.

a dog in the manger; dog days

Someone who is said to be behaving like *a dog in the manger* is a person who selfishly does not give others the things that he himself or she herself cannot use or enjoy. The expression comes from Aesop's fable of a dog who lay in a manger full of hay and growled at an ox who wanted to eat the hay, in spite of the fact that the dog did not want to eat it himself. The expression is often used in front of a noun: *a dog-in-the-manger attitude*.

Dog days are the hottest days of the year, a period marked by lazy inactivity. The expression goes back to classical times: the hottest six weeks or so of a Roman summer were known as the *dies caniculares*, days of the dog. This description arose from the theory that the heat from the rising of the dog star Sirius (from early July to mid-August) combined with the heat of the sun to give the hottest weather of the year.

doldrums (in the doldrums)

If an activity is described as being *in the doldrums*, it is inactive or depressed – nothing much is happening. The expression derives from the *doldrums*, a part of the ocean near the equator where calm conditions prevail. In this area, the north-east and south-east trade winds come together. Winds are calm or light but there may be sudden squalls and storms. Navigation by sailing-ship was difficult in the doldrums, with ships often remaining motionless for days.

dollar

The basic monetary unit in such countries as the USA, Canada, and Australia is the *dollar*. The word *dollar* comes from the name of the town *Sankt Joachimsthal* ('the valley of St Joachim') in Bohemia, now Jackymov in Czechoslovakia.

Silver coins were minted there in the early 16th century; a coin being known as *joachimsthaler* – which soon was shortened to *thaler*. This became *daler* in Dutch and Low German, from which is derived the English word *dollar*.

a doubting Thomas

A *doubting Thomas* is someone who is sceptical, particularly someone who refuses to believe until he or she has seen proof of something or has been otherwise satisfied as to its truth. The expression alludes to one of Jesus' apostles, *Thomas*, who refused to believe in Christ's resurrection until he had seen and felt Christ's body for himself (John 20: 24–29).

draconian

Draconian laws, measures, or regulations are very harsh or severe ones. The word comes from *Draco*, the 7th-century BC Athenian law-giver. In 621 BC he drew up what was probably the first comprehensive code of laws in Athens; before that time the laws had been interpreted arbitrarily by members of the city's governing body. Draco's code of laws was so severe – almost every named crime carried the death sentence – that *draconian* came to be used to describe laws of unreasonable cruelty. In 590 BC the Athenian statesman Solon issued a more lenient legal code.

dressed to the nines

To be *dressed to the nines* is to wear very smart clothes – for a party or other special occasion. The expression may derive from the Old English form dressed to *then eyne*, dressed to the eyes – or fashionably dressed from head to toe. Over the years the *n* shifted position to give our modern number *nine*. An alternative explanation suggests the use of *nine* as a mystical number representing finality, completion, or perfection.

a drop in the ocean/bucket

If something is described as *a drop in the ocean* or *a drop in the bucket*, it is very small when compared with something larger that is required, *£10 is just a drop in the ocean – the aim for the castle restoration fund is £500,000!* The origin of the expression is the Authorized (King James) Version of the Bible, Isaiah 40:15: 'Behold, the nations are as a drop of a bucket, and are counted as the small dust of the balance: behold, he taketh up the isles as a very little thing.' In other words, earthly countries are insignificant when compared with the greatness of God.

duffel

A *duffel* coat (or *duffle* coat) is a heavy coat of coarse woollen cloth, usually with a hood, and fastened with toggles. The coat takes its name from *Duffel*, a town near Antwerp in Belgium where such coats were first made, in the 17th century. The word later came to be applied to duffel bags, cylindrical bags for personal items, now made of canvas.

dunce

The word *dunce*, a person who is stupid or slow to learn, derives originally from the name of the Scottish theologian John *Duns* Scotus (c.1265–1308). A Franciscan, his teaching combined elements of Aristotle's and Augustine's doctrines, but he was opposed to the theology of St Thomas Aquinas. His teachings ('Scotism') were accepted by the Franciscans and were influential in the Middle Ages but were ridiculed in the 16th century by humanists and reformers who considered his followers (called *Dunsmen* or *Dunses*) reluctant to accept new theological ideas. The word *dunce* then came to refer to a person resistant to new ideas, hence to someone who is dull or stupid.

dungarees

The one-piece work overalls or trousers with a bib front made of coarse cotton cloth are known as *dungarees*, after the cloth, *dungaree*, from which they are made. *Dungaree* derives from Hindi *Dungrī*, the local name for the district in Bombay where the cloth (*dungrī*) was first sold.

the Dunkirk spirit

If a group of people are showing the *Dunkirk spirit*, they show courage and determination, and do not allow themselves to despair in a crisis. The allusion is to *Dunkerque* (Dunkirk) in northern France where in 1940 the British army was in such a position that only surrender or evacuation was possible. Mass evacuation of about 345,000 British and Allied troops was made possible by the resolute efforts of not only the armed forces but also large numbers of private boatowners who sailed from England to Dunkirk.

Dutch

The word *Dutch* is found in several expressions that have overtones of disrespect. Such expressions include: *double Dutch*, gibberish; *Dutch courage*, (false) courage gained from drinking alcohol; *Dutch treat*, a meal or entertainment at which those present pay for themselves, i.e. one that is not a treat at all, and thus *go Dutch*, to share costs or expenses equally; *talk like a Dutch uncle*, to speak bluntly, especially to criticize someone sternly and frankly. Why all these bad references to the Dutch? The explanation is found in the 17th century trading and colonial rivalries between Britain and the Netherlands. Although such hostility has long since disappeared, the rivalry has left its mark on the language.

dyed in the wool

Dyed in the wool, meaning having very strong uncompromising opinions, comes from the language of textiles. It was discovered that yarn that was dyed 'in the wool' – before being woven – retained its colour better than yarn that was dyed 'in the piece', i.e. after being woven. So from the literal dyed-in-the-wool came the figurative sense of dyed-in-the-wool beliefs as being those that were unlikely to change.

E

earmark

If something is *earmarked* for a specific purpose, it is set aside for that purpose: *A sum of money has been earmarked for use in possible emergencies.* The expression derives from the traditional practice of animal breeders putting a special identifying mark in the ears of their cattle and sheep to indicate ownership and so prevent theft.

earwig

An *earwig* is a small insect that has a pair of pincers at the end of its body. The name of the insect comes from the Old English *ēarwicga*, from *ēare*, ear, and *wicga*, insect or beetle. It is so called because of the old popular superstition that the insect crawled into the ear of people who were asleep and then bored its way through to the brain. The *wig* element of the word may also be related to *wiggle*. The insect has similar names in other languages: French *perce-oreille*, literally 'ear-piercer' and German *Ohrwurm*, 'ear-worm'.

easel

An *easel* is a wooden frame that supports a blackboard or an artist's canvas. The word, deriving from the Dutch *ezel*, ass or donkey, came to denote the supporting frame, since both animal and frame have the same function – to bear a load. A similar sense development can be seen in the English *horse* and *clothes-horse*, a frame for hanging wet clothes on to dry.

Easter

Easter, the name of the festival that marks the resurrection of Christ, has its origins in the name of the pagan goddess *Eostre*. Eostre was the Germanic goddess of the dawn and the ancient festival held in her honour took place at the spring equinox. Christian missionaries to England, anxious to make a smooth transition from paganism to Christianity, adopted the name (ēastre) of the pagan festival for the celebration of Christ's resurrection.

The practice of giving eggs at Easter also points to the festival's pagan origins. Eggs, symbolizing fertility and the rebirth of spring, were exchanged as gifts in ancient spring festivals. Christians adopted the egg to represent new life in Christ. This was convenient, because the number of eggs available increased during Lent, the period in which people were forbidden to eat them. So hens' eggs, hoarded for the Easter festivities, were carefully decorated and given as presents at Easter.

eat humble pie

In medieval times *humble pie* was actually a *numble pie*, or because of mistaken division of the words, *an umble pie*. It was made of the heart, liver, and entrails of the deer, known as the *numbles*. This food was eaten by servants and hunters, while the lord of the manor and his noble guests were feasting on the much more desirable finest cuts of venison. The person eating *umble pie* was therefore inferior and this fact, together with the gradual confusion of the word *umble* with the totally unrelated word *humble*, gave rise to the present meaning of the phrase *eat humble pie*, to be made to be more apologetic or respectful by admitting that one has done something wrong.

eavesdropper

An *eavesdropper* is someone who secretly listens to private conversations. The *eaves* are the lower edges of an overhanging roof, and before the days of guttering and drainpipes their function was to allow rain to drip away from the house itself. The area of ground onto which the rain was deflected was known as the *eavesdrip* (later changed to *eavesdrop*). So the eavesdrip, preferably near a window, provided an ideal place to listen in secretly to what people inside the house were saying.

eccentric

A person who is *eccentric* has strange habits and behaves in an odd way. The word originally meant 'off centre' and derives ultimately from Greek *ex*, out of, and *kentron*, centre. The figurative usage comes from the word's original more technical applications to describe something that has a different centre (*an eccentric sphere*) or an off-centre point of support or something that does not follow a circular path (*an eccentric orbit*).

electricity

The form of energy known as *electricity* was known to the ancient Greeks. Static electricity, as a force that was produced by rubbing a piece of amber, was known to attract small pieces of straw and other light materials. It was from the Greek word for amber, *ēlektron*, that the word *electricity* was coined by the English scientist William Gilbert (1544–1603). Gilbert was noted for his pioneering work on magnetism, especially his treatise *De Magnete* (1600) and he has become known as the 'Father of electricity'. Other terms that Gilbert introduced into English include *electric force* and *magnetic pole*.

Elementary, my dear Watson!

The somewhat dated saying *Elementary, my dear Watson* is used with an explanation that makes something clear and is obvious to the speaker. The expression is attributed to the fictional detective Sherlock Holmes but is not to be found in any of Arthur Conan Doyle's stories. The following exchange between Watson and Holmes does, however, appear in 'The Crooked Man', in *The Memoirs of Sherlock Holmes* (1894): '"Excellent!" I [Dr Watson] cried. "Elementary," said he [Sherlock Holmes].'

eleven (*at the eleventh hour*)

If something happens *at the eleventh hour*, it occurs at the last possible moment – at a time that is almost but not quite too late: *They asked Hans at the eleventh hour to step in and conduct the orchestra in place of Louis Garvonni who had fallen ill.* The expression, biblical in origin, refers to the time of hiring of the final group of workers in Jesus' parable about the labourers in the vineyard (Matthew 20:1–16). In the parable, the workers who started work at the eleventh hour received the same wage as the various groups of workers who had started earlier.

end (*make ends meet*)

To *make ends meet* means that one has just enough money for one's needs – that one's expenditure is kept within the amount of money earned: *Most people find it difficult to make ends meet.* The phrase comes from the longer *make both ends meet*, an accounting expression of the 19th century. Assets and liabilities had to balance – to be equal or 'mete'. The expression may also refer to the balancing of the accounts at both ends of the year: in times of irregular income one still had to receive, from the beginning of the year through to the end, sufficient income for all of one's expenditure.

enthusiast

An *enthusiast* is someone who has a great liking for and interest in something: *He's a model-railway enthusiast.* The word originally referred to someone who was inspired by a god, from Greek *entheos*, inspired, from *en-*, in, and *theos*, god. So an enthusiast was originally someone who had a god-given spirit of fervour.

Epsom salts

Epsom salts is a white powder (magnesium sulphate) that is mixed with water and drunk as a laxative. The name of this medicinal preparation derives from the mineral-spring water at *Epsom*, Surrey, England. Mineral springs were discovered in Epsom in 1618, and in the 17th century the town became a popular spa, particularly for Londoners. Epsom is also noted for the Epsom Downs racecourse where the Derby and the Oaks horseraces are held.

esquire

The word *esquire* is used in the abbreviated form *Esq.* instead of *Mr* as a formal title in correspondence: *J.R. Handsworth, Esq.* The word came into English via Middle French *esquier*, squire or shield-bearer, ultimately from Latin *scutum*, shield. In medieval times, esquires bore knights' shields as a sort of apprenticeship to knighthood. Later the word came to be used to refer to men above the level of ordinary tradespeople but below the rank of knight. Gradually the term came to be used for leading citizens and as a general mark of respect for those who did not have a higher title. In Britain, the formal title *Esq.* remains in use on an envelope, etc., addressed to a man; in the USA the title is rarely used except when writing to a lawyer.

etiquette

The conventionally accepted principles of correct social or professional behaviour are known as *etiquette*: *It is not considered etiquette to smoke between courses at a formal meal.* The word derives from French *étiquette*, ticket. Such a ticket was formerly a card that was issued to those attending court. It contained instructions concerning the required dress and behaviour for court functions. From this sense, the word gradually came to refer to a general set of rules for social behaviour.

eureka

Eureka is an exclamation that is sometimes used to express triumph at discovering the answer to a problem or mystery. The exclamation is attributed to the Greek mathematician and scientist Archimedes (c.287–c.212 BC). Archimedes is well known for his discovery of the so-called Archimedes' principle – that when a body is immersed in a liquid its apparent loss of weight equals the weight of the water that is displaced. It is alleged that he discovered this while taking a bath; on noticing that his body displaced the water in his bath, he is said to have exclaimed, '*Eureka*!' (Greek *heurēka*, 'I have found [it]!'). His discovery enabled him to give a response to King Hiero II. The king had asked Archimedes to find out the amount of gold in a crown that had been made for him, since he suspected that it was not made of pure gold. Archimedes' discovery led him to realize that since gold was heavier than silver, a floating vessel holding a pure-gold crown would displace more water than one holding a crown made of mixed metals. His tests proved that the king had in fact been supplied with a crown made of gold and base metal.

exchequer

The *Exchequer* is the government department in charge of the country's revenue. The origin of the word *exchequer* is not *cheque* or *exchange* as might be supposed, but in Old French *eschequier*, chessboard. This was the name given to the cloth that covered the counting tables used by the Norman and Plantagenet kings of England. The cloth, marked off in squares, resembled a chessboard, with the kings and their assistants using coloured counters on it to work out the country's finances. The *ex-* spelling of our word *exchequer* lies in the association of the Old English *ex-*, as in *exchange*.

excruciating

Something that is *excruciating* is extremely painful. The origin of this word is Latin *excruciare*, to torture, from Latin *cruciare*, to crucify, and *crux*, cross. This shows that the Romans considered death by crucifixion as the most agonizing method of execution.

explode

If a bomb *explodes*, it bursts noisily and forcefully, often causing a lot of damage. The origin of the word lies in the theatre: to *explode* an actor meant to drive him or her off the stage by clapping – from Latin *ex-* out of, and *plaudere*, to clap or applaud. If an actor gave a performance of low quality, the audience went on clapping and hissing until he or she left the stage. The sense of rejecting also still survives in the word *explode*, in the meaning 'to destroy a belief or theory by showing it to be false'.

an eye for an eye

The phrase *an eye for an eye* is used to refer to punishment or harsh treatment that is expressed in the same way as the offence that has been committed. The saying, sometimes used to justify personal or even national retaliation in conflicts, comes from the Authorized (King James) Version of the Bible, Exodus 21:22–24: 'If men strive, and hurt a woman with child, so that her fruit depart from her, and yet no mischief follow: he shall be surely punished, according as the woman's husband will lay upon him; and he shall pay as the judges determine. And if any mischief follow, then thou shalt give life for life, eye for eye, tooth for tooth, hand for hand, foot for foot.'

F

face the music

If one has to *face the music*, one has to accept the unpleasant consequences – e.g. criticism or punishment – that are about to come because of one's actions. There are two explanations of the origin of this expression. Some authorities suggest that the derivation of the phrase lies in the theatre. A nervous actor or entertainer who comes on stage not only has to face the audience, but also has to *face the music* – the musicians in the orchestra pit in front of the stage. The other, more probable, explanation is that the phrase goes back to the military practice of drumming out a soldier – dismissing him from service for dishonourable behaviour. The expulsion took place to the accompaniment of the steady beating of drums.

farce

A *farce* is a humorous play that is based on improbable and ridiculous situations. The word has its origin in medieval times, when phrases were inserted in liturgical prayers such as the *kyrie eleison*. Such an inserted (or 'stuffed') phrase was called a *farsa* or *farcia*, from Latin *farcire*, to stuff. (This word is seen in a slightly changed form in the modern cookery term *forcemeat*.) Later, short comic jokes were introduced into the main text of religious dramas. From such brief additional humorous sections developed the sense of a whole play based on a series of unlikely and absurd situations, and in an extended sense, something very disorganized and ludicrous.

fast (play fast and loose with someone)

If one *plays fast and loose with someone*, one behaves in an irresponsible and deceitful way to him or her: *His mother warned him against playing fast and loose with a girl's affections*. The expression probably derives from an old fairground con trick. In this swindle, an operator arranged a belt so that a player thought he could push a skewer through the belt's folds, pinning it to the table. But the operator had folded the belt in such a way that when the player supposed he had held the belt tight, the operator would pull it to show that the belt was not really *fast*, but in fact *loose*. Thus the victim would be deceived and so lose the bet.

a feather in one's cap; feather one's nest

A *feather in one's cap* is an achievement for which other people respect one greatly and of which one can justifiably feel proud: *Winning such a contract so soon after joining the company was a real feather in her cap*. The phrase may well go back to the days when American Indian braves were given a feather to be put in their head-dress for every enemy warrior that they had killed. Such feathers therefore honoured brave accomplishments. An alternative explanation is that the feather was the plume of a heron, worn in the caps of brave Knights of the Garter.

To *feather one's nest* is to look after one's own financial interests, especially by being greedy or dishonest, in order to lead a comfortable life. The original reference is to the habits of birds lining their nests with down to ensure that they are soft and comfortable for themselves and their young.

fell (at one fell swoop)

If something happens *at* (or *in*) *one fell swoop*, it happens in a single concentrated action: *It'll be impossible to eliminate all the government subsidies at one fell swoop.* The *fell* in this phrase does not come from the verb *fall*, as might be supposed, but derives from Middle English *fel*, cruel, deadly, or ruthless (from which the word *felon* also comes). So when an eagle snatches its prey *at one fell swoop*, it leaps suddenly on to its victim and grabs it fiercely. The expression *at one fell swoop* is first found in Shakespeare's *Macbeth* (Act 4, Scene iii):

> All my pretty ones?
> Did you say all? O hell-kite! All?
> What! all my pretty chickens and their dam,
> At one fell swoop?

fiddle while Rome burns

If someone is said to be *fiddling while Rome burns*, he or she is doing nothing or behaving frivolously when urgent action is called for to meet a serious situation. The expression derives from the story that the Roman emperor Nero (Claudius Caesar, 37–68 AD) continued to play a musical instrument – probably a lute or lyre – and sung while he watched Rome being devastated by a fire that destroyed a large part of the city in 64 AD. It was alleged that Nero caused the fire, but he in fact blamed it on the Christians and fiercely persecuted that sect.

fifth column

A *fifth column* is a group of people that live in one country but secretly support and work for that country's enemy. The expression originated in 1936 during the Spanish Civil War (1936–39) when the Falangist General Emilio Mola (1887–1937) outside Madrid said that he had five columns attacking the city: four outside the city and a fifth column (Spanish *quinta columna*) of people already inside the city who were working secretly for him. (Other authorities attribute the expression to Lieutenant-General Queipo de Llano, 1875–1951). The expression *fifth column* was popularized in English by the title of the play by Ernest Hemingway (1938).

filibuster

A *filibuster* is the use of delaying tactics in a legislative assembly. The word derives from Spanish *filibustero*, a free-booter or pirate, originally from Dutch *vrijbuiter*, one who plunders freely. The first freebooters – private citizens who engaged in war against a nation with whom their own country was at peace – were gun-runners in the early 1850s. These adventurers were attempting to stir up revolution in Latin America. The first use of *filibuster* as a noun and a verb in the political sense of obstructing legislation in the US Senate came in 1853.

a fine kettle of fish

If a situation is described as being *a fine* (or *pretty*) *kettle of fish*, it is very confused or awkward. The expression is said to derive from the former custom found along the border between England and Scotland. As salmon began to move upstream to spawn each year, large outdoor picnics were held along the streams, the main course at such parties being salmon. The fish would be caught, boiled in a metal cooking pan (*kettle*), and eaten on the spot. When things went wrong, e.g. a kettle was upset or people burnt their fingers trying to eat freshly boiled salmon, *a pretty kettle of fish* – a scene of muddle and confusion – was the result.

flagstone

A *flagstone* is a large flat square piece of hard stone used for paving. The *flag* in this word has nothing to do with a banner, as might be thought, but comes from Middle English *flagge*, piece of turf, sod, and ultimately from Old Norse *flaga*, flake or slab of stone. So the original *flagstone* was a piece of hard stone 'flaked' into flat squares for paving – just as a turf is a piece cut out of the grass.

a flash in the pan

If something is described as *a flash in the pan* it is thought that its success is not likely to last a long time: *The player's first-rate performances early in the season turned out to be something of a flash in the pan, as they've not been so good since*. The expression goes back to the days of the flintlock musket. There was a flash in the pan when the trigger was pulled, and the sparks that were produced by the hammer striking a piece of flint caused the powder (in the *pan*) to flare up with a *flash*, but failed to explode the main charge. The promising start came to nothing in the end.

a fly in the ointment

A *fly in the ointment* is something that spoils a situation that is otherwise perfect or successful: *We had a great holiday. The only fly in the ointment was that Robert had a bad cold for the first few days*. The expression comes from the Authorized (King James) Version of the Bible, Ecclesiastes 10:1: 'Dead flies cause the ointment of the apothecary to send forth a stinking savour.'

foolscap

Foolscap is a large size of paper, especially 13½ inches by 17 inches (343 mm × 432 mm). The paper is so named because it formerly bore the watermark of a *fool's* head and *cap*.

foot *(have one foot in the grave)*

If someone is said to *have one foot in the grave,* he or she is very ill or old and is on the point of dying or likely to die soon. The origin of the expression is generally attributed to the Roman emperor Julian the Apostate (Flavius Claudius Julianus, 331–363 AD). Julian is alleged to have said, 'I will learn this even if I have one foot in the grave'. A similar expression is found in Greek mythology: *with one foot in Charon's ferry-boat,* Charon being the name of the ferryman who transported the dead in his boat across the River Styx to the blessed Elysian fields.

forlorn hope

The phrase *a forlorn hope* is used to refer to a difficult undertaking that almost certainly will not be realized: *the forlorn hope of achieving full employment, zero inflation, and a balance-of-payments surplus.* The expression comes from Dutch *verloren hoop,* literally 'a lost band of troops'. This phrase was originally used to refer to a small group of assault troops who were sent on a dangerous mission in advance of the main forces. The small group were seen as expendable, as they had little chance of returning alive. Although the Dutch words *verloren hoop* do not mean 'forlorn hope', it was popularly thought that these English words sounded like the Dutch phrase, and so the expression came into English.

freelance

A *freelance* is someone who does not have a long-term contract with one employer but receives pay for the different items of work undertaken for various organizations: *a freelance writer, photographer*, etc. The word originally referred to a medieval mercenary who was willing to hire out his skills in combat with a *lance* to any cause. Their lance was *free*, not in the sense that they made no charge for their services but that they were free of any long-term loyalty to one particular master. So they were available to take up arms for whoever paid the most.

G

the game isn't worth the candle

If you say that *the game isn't worth the candle* you mean that the results gained from doing something are not worth the effort or cost involved. One explanation of this phrase alludes to the days of playing gambling games by candlelight. To a player who was losing, the game was obviously not worth even the price of the candle.

gamut

The *gamut* of something is the whole range: *Her feelings ran the full gamut of emotion – from horror to sorrow to ecstasy and joy.* The word *gamut* comes from *gamma* and *ut*, the lowest note in the musical scale established by the 11th-century monk and musical theorist Guido d'Arezzo. *Gamma* was the lowest note of the scale, bottom G of our modern bass clef. The first note of the scale (our modern *doh*) was known as *ut*, the other five being *re, mi, fa, sol*, and *la*. These six notes came from the first syllables of six lines of a Latin hymn to St John the Baptist. So the lowest note came to be known as *gamma ut*, abbreviated to *gamut*. *Gamut* then became a handy way of referring to the whole range of notes and, figuratively, an entire sequence.

garlic

Garlic is the small bulbous root of an onion-like plant, has a very strong aroma and taste, and is used as a flavouring in cooking. The word goes back to Old English *gārlēac*, from a joining of the words *gār*, spear and *lēac*, leek, from the fact that the leaves of the garlic plant were thought to resemble spear heads.

gauntlet (*run the gauntlet*)

To *run the gauntlet* is to go through an unpleasant experience in which many people criticize one. Running the gauntlet referred originally to a form of military punishment that became prominent, so it seems, in the Thirty Years' War (1618–48). The *gauntlet* (from Swedish *gatlopp*, from *gata*, road and *lop*, course) consisted of two lines of men who faced each other and who would attack with clubs, whips, or other weapons an individual who was forced to run between them.

gauntlet (*throw down the gauntlet*)

The *gauntlet* in the expression *throw down the gauntlet* has an origin that is different from that of the *gauntlet* of the previous entry. Here, the *gauntlet* (from Middle French *gant*, glove) was originally a heavy leather or steel glove which was worn as part of a knight's armour. (Today's gauntlets are heavy protective gloves with a long cuff.) When one knight *threw down the gauntlet* to another, he was challenging him to a duel. If the second knight picked up the gauntlet, he was showing that he had accepted the challenge – he was agreeing that the fight should take place. Today, both *throw down the gauntlet* and *pick up* (or *take up*) *the gauntlet* are used figuratively to mean 'to issue a challenge' and 'to accept such a challenge' respectively.

gazette

The word *gazette* is sometimes used as the title of a newspaper or official journal, e.g. *Botanical Gazette, UK Press Gazette*. There are two theories of the origin of the word. Some authorities suggest that the word derives from Italian *gazeta*, a small copper coin that in the Venice of 16th century was the cost of buying the government newspaper. An alternative explanation is that the word is a diminutive of *gazza*, magpie – perhaps because the news-sheet was filled with the chatter that is commonly associated with the bird.

ghost (*give up the ghost*)

The expression *give up the ghost*, meaning 'to die', alludes to the belief that life exists independently of the physical human body and that at death the *ghost* (soul) of a person leaves the body and continues to live. The expression goes back at least to the Authorized (King James) Version of the Bible, e.g. Job 14.10: 'But man dieth, and wasteth away: yea, man giveth up the ghost, and where is he?' *Ghost* in the sense of 'spirit' is still seen in the name *Holy Ghost*, the Holy Spirit.

gift (*the gift of the gab; not look a gift horse in the mouth*)

If it is said that someone has the *gift of the gab*, he or she can talk effortlessly, confidently, and persuasively. The *gab* here may come from the northern English dialectal (and slang) *gob*, mouth. Alternatively, *gab* may derive from *gabble*, foolish chatter, from Middle Dutch *gabbelen*.

The expression *Don't look a gift horse in the mouth* means that one should not complain or be critical about something that is offered at no cost. The saying is an old one, a Latin version of it appearing in a work by St Jerome in the 5th century AD.

The origin of the expression lies in the tradition that the age of a horse can be estimated by inspecting its teeth. But if someone were to make a *gift* of a *horse*, it would be disrespectful to *look in its mouth* to see how old it was. Thus, figuratively, one should not be too critical about what is freely given. See also LONG IN THE TOOTH.

gild the lily

To *gild the lily* means to spoil something that is already attractive by adding unnecessary improvements to it. The expression is in fact a misquotation from Shakespeare's *King John* (Act 4, Scene ii).

> To *gild* refined gold, to paint *the lily*,
> To throw a perfume on the violet,
> To smooth the ice, or add another hue
> Unto the rainbow, or with taper light
> To seek the beauteous eye of heaven to garnish,
> Is wasteful and ridiculous excess.

goat (get someone's goat)

If something *gets someone's goat*, it annoys him or her greatly. The expression is said to come from the language of the race course. In former times, a goat was sometimes stabled with an excitable horse in an effort to keep the horse calm. If however someone *got* (ran off with) the horse's *goat* the night before a big race, the horse would clearly become upset and perform very badly on the racetrack. The result: a ruffled horse whose goat had been got (literally) and the angry horse's owner whose goat had been got (figuratively speaking).

a good Samaritan

A *good Samaritan* is someone who helps others in need. The phrase refers to the parable that Jesus told of the Samaritan who rescued and helped an injured man who had been attacked and robbed – when two 'holy' men had passed by on the other side without offering any help at all. In the story (Luke 10:30–37), the man from Samaria is nameless; he is described simply as 'a *Samaritan*', but his kind and selfless actions are remembered in the expression *a good Samaritan* that has long been part of the language.

The *Samaritans* is also the name of a telephone service which was established in Britain in 1953. It provides a confidential and anonymous service to anyone in despair.

gossamer

Gossamer is the light fine film of cobwebs on bushes, etc., or any fine delicate material. The word derives from Middle English *gosesomer*, from *gos* goose and *somer* summer. This was the name (also known as *St Martin's summer*) given to an unseasonably warm and pleasant period of weather in autumn, a time of year at which geese were traditionally ready to be eaten. So the filmy cobwebs floating in the air in this clear calm weather came to be associated with geese – hence 'goose summer'.

gossip

The Old English word from which *gossip* derives is *godsibb*, originally 'a godparent', from *God* plus *sibb*, 'relation'. Gossips were the sponsors for children at baptism – Shakespeare in *Two Gentlemen of Verona* wrote: ''Tis not a maid, for she hath had gossips' (Act 3, Scene i). Gradually the word came to be applied to familiar friends and acquaintances, and then to the contemporary sense of someone fond of idle talk. Interestingly, the Old English *sibb* is preserved in the modern word *sibling*, a person's brother or sister.

grace (*there but for the grace of God, go I*)

The expression *there but for the grace of God, go I* is used when commenting on someone who is in an unfortunate situation (e.g. suffering punishment for a foolish action) and stating that one could well have been in the same situation if God had not acted kindly towards one or if one's circumstances were not as favourable as they are. The saying derives from the quotation by the English Protestant martyr John Bradford (c.1510–55). As Bradford saw some criminals being led to execution, he remarked, 'There, but for the grace of God, goes John Bradford'. Bradford himself was burnt at the stake at Smithfield, London for alleged heresy.

Greek (*all Greek to me*)

If one says, '*It's all Greek to me,*' one means that something is completely beyond one's understanding. The expression is nowadays applied to specialist language or speech or writing that is unintelligible. The phrase derives from Shakespeare's *Julius Caesar* (Act 1, Scene ii): 'For mine own part, it was Greek to me.' The words are those of Casca, one of the conspirators against Caesar, speaking about Cicero's remarks after Caesar refused the crown of king three times. Cicero in fact spoke in Greek, to ensure that passers-by did not understand him.

the green-eyed monster

The *green-eyed monster* is jealousy. The phrase derives from Shakespeare's *Othello* (Act 3, Scene iii):

> O! beware, my lord, of jealousy;
> It is the green-ey'd monster which doth mock
> The meat it feeds on.

The reference here is to (green-eyed) cats toying with their victims before killing and eating them. In the same way jealousy, with its mixed emotions of love and hatred, may 'consume' people in their desire to have or keep what they consider to be their own.

grin like a Cheshire cat

To *grin like a Cheshire cat* is to have a broad (sometimes foolish) smile on one's face. The phrase is familiar from Lewis Carroll's *Alice's Adventures in Wonderland* (1865), in which a Cheshire cat vanishes – except for its grin, which remains visible. The origin of the expression does not lie with Carroll, however. It is possible that at one time cheeses made in this English county were moulded in the form of grinning cats. Other authorities suggest that the coat of arms of one of Cheshire's great families bore a lion, which, when represented by ignorant sign painters, came in the course of time to have the appearance of a grinning cat.

guerrilla

Guerrilla (also sometimes spelt *guerilla*) comes originally from Spanish, in which it means 'little war'. The word was first used to refer to the irregular way that the Spanish-Portuguese resistance movement fought against Napoleon's armies in the

Peninsular War (1808–14). Nowadays *guerrillas* (e.g. *urban guerrillas*) or those who engage in *guerrilla warfare* are members of small independent armed units who engage in sabotage, harassment, etc., against their enemy, specially in an attempt to gain political support for their cause.

gypsy

Gypsies (or *gipsies*) are a people who travel from place to place in caravans. The people are so named because in the 16th century it was thought that they came from Egypt and so were called *Egyptians* – which gradually became shortened and altered to its present form. In fact, gypsies probably originally came from north-west India, migrating first to what was then Persia and, in the 14th to 16th centuries, to Europe.

H

ha-ha

A *ha-ha* is a sudden vertical drop, a 'sunken fence' that marks a boundary. Ha-has were used in the 18th century in grounds and parks as a landscape-gardening device, as they did not interrupt the view from a house of the countryside beyond. The name is said to derive from the surprise of people strolling round the grounds and unexpectedly coming across the drop. Their amazement was expressed as 'Ha-ha!' and so the exclamation was used as the name of the ditch.

halcyon

Halcyon days are those that are peaceful and remembered as being happy ones. The word *halcyon* derives from Greek *halkyōn*, kingfisher. Legend had it that kingfishers bred during the period seven days before and seven days after the winter solstice (21 December). At this time, the kingfisher was said to build a nest that floated on the sea – in waters that were calm and peaceful, or in other words *halcyon*.

hallmark

A *hallmark* is an official mark that is stamped on articles of gold or silver to show that their purity has been tested. The word derives from Goldsmiths *Hall* in London, where gold and silver articles were assayed and stamped from 1300 onwards. Each article bears the marks of the assay office, a mark guaranteeing quality, a date mark, and a maker's mark. The word *hallmark* has also acquired the figurative sense of a typical quality or distinguishing feature: *the wry sense of humour that was the entertainer's hallmark.*

hammer and tongs

If someone is going at something *hammer and tongs,* he or she is acting very forcefully. The phrase is particularly used of people engaged in a violent argument: *The two sides in the row over the new road are really going at each other hammer and tongs.* The allusion is to the traditional work of the blacksmith: he would hold the hot metal taken from the forge with a pair of *tongs* (long-handled pincers) and vigorously and loudly beat the iron into shape with a *hammer.*

hangnail

A *hangnail* is a piece of skin that hangs loose at the side or base of a fingernail. The Old English word from which *hangnail* comes is *angnægl,* a corn on the toe, from *ang,* pain and *nægl,* nail – from the resemblance of a corn to the head of a nail. The unfamiliar *ang* was thought to be the more familiar *hang,* and the meaning became transferred from the foot to the finger – hence the name *hangnail* for the irritating and painful piece of cuticle.

harbinger

A *harbinger* is a thing or person that announces or shows the coming of something: *a harbinger of good news.* This rather literary term has its origins in Old French *herbergere*, related to Old High German *heriberga*, army shelter from *hari*, army, and *bergan*, to lodge. The original *harbinger* was a person who provided or secured lodgings for soldiers. Later, it came to describe a person sent ahead of a group of travellers, e.g. such as troops or a royal party, to arrange their accommodation. Subsequently, *harbinger* came to refer to anyone who is a forerunner – who goes forward to announce the approach of something.

havoc

Havoc, destruction or disorder (*the havoc caused by the hurricane*), comes from Anglo-French *havok*. This was a war cry – a signal to invaders to attack and plunder indiscriminately and without mercy. The expression *cry havoc* comes from Shakespeare's *Julius Caesar* (Act 3, Scene i):

> ... Caesar's spirit, ranging for revenge,
> With Atè by his side come hot from hell,
> Shall in these confines with a monarch's voice
> Cry, '*Havoc*!' and let slip the dogs of war.

haywire (go haywire)

The idiomatic phrase *go haywire* means to go out of control or become completely disorganized: *The computer seems to have gone absolutely haywire – it's been printing out utter nonsense all morning*! The allusion is to the wire used by farmers to bind and bale hay. This would often become twisted and, when cut, would fly around in an unpredictable and dangerous manner. The disorder created by the use of such wire is the source of the phrase.

hell (all hell breaks loose)

The expression *all hell breaks loose* refers to a state of terrible uproar, violent reactions and noisy anger, etc. The origin of the phrase is Milton's *Paradise Lost* (Book 4) and the archangel Gabriel's taunt to Satan:

> But wherefore thou alone? Where with thee
> Came not all hell broke loose?

helpmate

A *helpmate* is a companion and helper, particularly a wife or husband. The word is a misquotation of the text of the Authorized (King James) Version of the Bible, Genesis 2:18: 'And the LORD God said, It is not good that the man should be alone; I will make him an help meet for him.' The word *meet* meant 'suitable', and the whole phrase that God intended to create a fitting help for man. The two words *help meet* were constantly run together when read aloud to give the single word *helpmeet* and later this word became changed to *helpmate* as it was thought that this seemed more comprehensible.

hide one's light under a bushel

To *hide one's light under a bushel* is to conceal one's talents or abilities from other people: *We never knew you could play the guitar, Sandy – you've been hiding your light under a bushel!* The phrase comes from the words of Jesus in the Sermon on the Mount, as recorded in the Authorized (King James) Version of the Bible, Matthew 5:15: 'Neither do men light a candle, and put it under a bushel, but on a candlestick; and it giveth light unto all that are in the house.' The purpose of a light is to illuminate its surroundings, and so it is therefore useless to put it under a *bushel*. A bushel was an earthenware or wooden bowl that was used to measure dry materials to a capacity equivalent to 8.75 litres.

hobnob

To *hobnob* with someone is to associate in a friendly manner with him or her: *There he goes again, hobnobbing with royalty!* The word *hobnob* was found in Shakespeare's plays, and was originally *hab* or *nab*, hit or miss, have or have not. The term was used to refer to the taking in turns of buying drinks: someone buys one round, with his friend buying the next. From this drinking 'give and take' developed the meaning of engaging in any kind of social familiarity and mixing.

Hobson's choice

If one is faced with *Hobson's choice*, one is in a situation in which there appear to be alternatives. In reality, however, no real choice is offered and there is only one thing that one can do. The expression derives from the liveryman Thomas *Hobson* (1544–1631) of Cambridge, England. He is said not to have allowed his customers any right to pick one particular horse, insisting that they always choose the horse that was nearest the door when they arrived. It is said that Hobson acted in this way so that no horse was overworked: by taking each horse in strict rotation, each horse was used equally.

hog (*go the whole hog*)

To *go the whole hog* is to do something completely: *We've decorated the living room – why don't we go the whole hog and paint the hall and stairs as well?* There are two theories of the origin of this idiomatic expression. According to one theory, a *hog* was a shilling in 17th-century England, obviously worth a lot more than its equivalent (5 pence) is worth today. So *to go the whole hog* meant to be extravagant and spend a lot of money at once.

The other explanation refers to the poem *The Love of the World Reproved; or Hypocrisy Detected* (1779) by the English poet William Cowper (1731–1800). The poem describes the difficulty experienced by Muslims in deciding what part of the hog they were prohibited by Mohammed from eating:

> But for one piece they thought it hard
> From the whole hog to be debarr'd;
> And set their wit at work to find
> What joint the prophet had in mind ...
> Thus, conscience freed from ev'ry clog,
> Mahometans eat up the hog ...
> With sophistry their sauce they sweeten,
> 'Til quite from tail to snout 'tis eaten.

hoist by one's own petard

To be *hoist by one's own petard* means that one becomes the victim of one's own plans to harm others. In the Middle Ages, a *petard* was an explosive devise used to breach the gates or walls of an enemy's castle. To lay such a device was a risky operation, and since the charges were not always well put together, the slow-burning fuse sometimes exploded prematurely. In such instances, not only the castle wall or gate but also the man laying the fuse was blown sky-high, or literally *hoisted* (raised) *by his own petard*. Shakespeare used the phrase (although in a slightly different form) in *Hamlet* (Act 3, Scene iv):

> For 'tis the sport to have the engineer
> Hoist with his own petar: and it shall go hard
> But I will delve below their mines,
> And blow them at the moon.

This usage has undoubtedly ensured that the expression — now used figuratively — has remained in the language.

113

holocaust

A *holocaust* is great destruction and loss of life: *the threat of a nuclear holocaust*. Often written with a capital letter, *the Holocaust* stands for the murder of European Jews by the Nazis during World War II. A *holocaust* was originally a pre-Christian sacrificial offering that was consumed by fire – a whole burnt offering, the word coming from Greek *holokaustos*, burnt whole, from Greek *holos*, whole, and *kaustos*, burnt (compare our modern *caustic*). From this developed a more general (and now archaic) sense of sacrifice and later, separately, the sense of destruction on a large-scale, especially by fire.

honeymoon

A *honeymoon* is a holiday taken by a newly married couple. There are several different explanations of the origin of the word. Some authorities refer to the ancient Germanic tradition of the newly wed husband and wife drinking mead (fermented *honey* and water) for the 30 days (*moon*) after their wedding. It is even said that Attila, king of the Huns, suffocated himself in 453 AD during his wedding banquet as he drank too much of the potion. Other authorities point to the waxing and waning of the *moon* and see in that a reflection of the changing affections of the newlyweds: a love that grows at first but declines later. Still others see in the word a simpler comparison: the sweetness of *honey* and the romantic happiness of *moon*light.

hook, line, and sinker

To believe something *hook, line, and sinker* is to accept it completely: *It doesn't seem possible now, but at the time we fell for his hard-luck story hook, line, and sinker*. The allusion is to angling: a hungry fish swallows not only the *hook* with the bait, but also the *line* and *sinker* (weight) of the fishing-tackle as well.

It generally implies a deception, and when the deception is complete.

on the horns of a dilemma

Medieval philosophers held that a *dilemma* (from Greek *di*, two and *lēmma*, thing taken, assumption) was an argument in which a person had to choose between two alternatives, each of which was unfavourable to him. The two alternatives were compared to an animal's horns, as no matter which horn was seized, one risked being painfully tossed up in the air by the animal. So to be caught *on the horns of a dilemma* is to be unable to decide which of two difficult courses of action to choose.

hue and cry

A *hue and cry* is an angry public outcry: *the hue and cry that followed the announcement that the hospital was to be closed.* The phrase dates back to the 16th century, when it referred to a loud cry uttered in pursuit of a suspected criminal in order to raise the alarm. Those hearing the shouts were legally obliged to join in the chase. The expression comes from Anglo-French *hu et cri*, (from Old French *hue*,) *hu* was an exclamation warning of danger and *cri*, was to cry.

husband

The word *husband* at one time referred to a man's economic status, rather than his marital status. In the Middle Ages, a *husband* was the master or manager of a household, regardless of whether he was married. *Husband* derives from Old Norse *hūs*, house, and *bōndi*, householder. The sense of managing is retained in the verb, as in: *to husband the nation's economic resources.*

hustings

The word *hustings* is used to refer to the activities of a political campaign before an election: *a programme of tonight's speeches from the hustings.* Until 1872, this was the name given to the platform on which candidates for Parliament were nominated and from which they delivered their speeches to the electors. But hustings goes back even further: an Anglo-Saxon *hūsting* was an assembly summoned by a king, earl, etc., the word itself coming from Old Norse *hūs*, house, and *thing*, assembly or council.

hysteria

Hysteria is the medical term for a mental disorder marked by emotional instability and some physical symptoms, or in more general language use, a state of intense uncontrolled excitement shown, e.g. in fits of laughter or weeping. The word comes from Greek *hystera*, womb, since it was formerly believed that hysteria in women was caused by disorders of the womb.

I

idiot

The present meaning of *idiot* is a fool – someone who has done something very stupid. But originally the word had no derogatory overtones. The word comes from Greek *idiōtēs*, private person, from *idios*, one's own, from which we also have such words as *idiom* and *idiosyncrasy*. So originally an *idiot* was one who held no public office or had no professional knowledge – what we would call a layman. But since it was only the intelligent educated people who were qualified to take up appointments of public office, the word gradually came to refer to a person who was unsuitable for such a post because of his general ignorance. In due course such a weakness became linked with mental, rather than educational, deficiency and thus *idiot* came to refer to an imbecile or fool.

ignorance is bliss

The expression *ignorance is bliss* is sometimes used to justify one's lack of knowledge of something. The phrase derives from

Ode on a Distant Prospect of Eton College (1747) by the English poet Thomas Gray (1716–71):

> Yet ah! why should they know their fate?
> Since sorrow never comes too late,
> And happiness too swiftly flies.
> Thought would destroy their paradise.
> No more; where ignorance is bliss,
> 'Tis folly to be wise.

In the original, Gray is making a wistful comment about carefree, untroubled youth.

imp

In Old English, an *imp* was a young offshoot of a tree. As a verb, to *imp* meant to graft on new shoots. In the 14th century came the metaphorical development from 'offshoot' to 'offspring or child'. Two centuries later the word became used in such expressions as *the imp of Satan* and *the Devil's imp* to refer to a little demon or evil spirit – hence the idea of a mischievous child conveyed by the modern use of the word.

inch (*give someone an inch and he'll take a mile*)

The modern phrase was originally *give someone an inch and he'll take an ell* deriving from Old English *eln*, forearm. An *ell* was originally the measurement of the distance from the elbow to the fingertips, which obviously varied in length from person to person, but which came to be reckoned to be 45 centimetres. So the expression means that if one grants slight concessions to someone, then he or she will make much greater demands on one or generally act in an excessive manner.

influenza

Influenza is a virus disease that is characterized by chills, fever, aches and pains, and catarrh. The word came via Italian from Latin *influentia*, influence. In contemporary English when the word *influence* is used to refer to illness, it usually refers to drink: *driving under the influence* is a polite way of stating that someone is driving while drunk. In former times, however, when people were suffering from *influenza*, they were suffering not from the effects of alcohol, but, according to superstition, from the evil effects of the stars. The word was first applied to the epidemic that broke out in Italy in 1743 and, like other epidemics, was thought to have been caused by astrological influences. The disease spread throughout Europe including England, where the Italian word was borrowed and anglicized to give *influenza*, which in due course became shortened to *flu*.

intelligentsia

The word *intelligentsia* is used to refer to the intellectual group of people in society – those interested in the cultural arts, politics, etc. The word comes ultimately from Latin *intelligentia*, perceptiveness or understanding. The word was taken over into Italian, from where, curiously, it was borrowed by Russia to refer to those who, in pre-revolutionary times, 'aspired to intellectual activity' (*Oxford English Dictionary*, 2nd edition) in Russian society. The word was taken over into English in the first quarter of the 20th century.

iron (*Iron Curtain; have many irons in the fire*)

The phrase the *Iron Curtain* is used to refer to the limit of the range of influence of the Soviet Union: the strongly guarded border between the Communist countries of eastern Europe (that come within the Soviet Union's orbit) and western Europe. The expression is popularly believed to have originated with Winston Churchill's speech on 5 March 1946 at Fulton, Missouri, 'From Stettin, in the Baltic, to Trieste, in the Adriatic, an iron curtain has descended across the Continent.' Various earlier quotations of the phrase have been cited, e.g. 1920 by Mrs P. Snowden, *Through Bolshevik Russia*, writing of her arrival in Petrograd, 'We were behind the "iron curtain" at last!' The phrase is an extension of the sense 'an impenetrable barrier', itself a figurative application of the expression as used to refer to the fireproof iron curtain in a theatre, which can be lowered between the stage and the auditorium. The phrase *bamboo curtain* was later coined to refer to the political and military barrier around the territories controlled by Communist China.

The expression *have many irons in the fire* means that one has several different plans or that one is participating in several different activities at the same time: '*I didn't get the job I went for, but at least I've got a few other irons in the fire.*' The phrase most probably derives from the blacksmith's forge. If the smith was heating many pieces of iron in his fire, he was working on several different jobs at the same time.

italic

Printed letters that slant upward to the right are known as *italics*. Italic type was invented by the Italian printer Aldus Manutius (1450–1515), who modelled the style on elegant handwriting. The type was first used in a publication of an edition of Virgil printed by Manutius' so-called *Aldine Press* in

Venice and published in 1501, Manutius dedicating the work to his native Italy. Because of this dedication, the new slanting type became known as *italic*, from Latin *Italicus*, of Italy.

itching palm

To have an *itching* (or *itchy*) *palm* means to be greedy, especially for money. The phrase, which alludes to the superstition that if the palm of one's hand was itching, one was going to receive money, dates back at least to Shakespeare's time. The expression occurs in *Julius Caesar* (Act 4, Scene iii):

Let me tell you, Cassius, you yourself
Are much condemn'd to have an itching palm.

Ivy League

The *Ivy League* is a group of eight colleges in the eastern part of the USA: Brown, Columbia, Cornell, Dartmouth, Harvard, the University of Pennsylvania, Princeton, and Yale, regarded as having high academic and social prestige. The term, referring to the fact that many of the colleges' buildings are ivy-covered, is generally accepted to have been coined by Caswell Adams, US sportswriter on the *New York Herald Tribune* in the mid-1930s. At that time the football team of Fordham University was among the best in the country. When a colleague compared the teams of Columbia and Princeton to Fordham, Adams answered that the first two were 'just Ivy League', later writing that he had said this 'with complete disparagement in mind'. Stanley Woodward, the sports editor, noted the comment and used it the following day.

J

jam tomorrow

The phrase *jam tomorrow* is used to refer to the promise of better working or living conditions in the future, a promise that may not in reality be fulfilled. The expression comes from *Through the Looking-Glass* by Lewis Carroll: 'The rule is, jam tomorrow and jam yesterday – but never jam today.'

jeep

A *jeep* is a small robust motor vehicle with four-wheel drive. The name is probably an altered form of the initials *GP*, standing for *g*eneral-*p*urpose (vehicle), the vehicle's code designation. It seems certain that the general acceptance of the word can be attributed largely to the popularity of the character, Eugene the Jeep, introduced in the syndicated comic strip *Popeye* created by the US cartoonist Elzie Crisler Segar (1894–1938) in 1936. Eugene the Jeep made the peeping sound, 'Jeep, jeep,' and could do nearly anything.

jeopardy

If something is in *jeopardy*, it is at risk: *Their lack of response puts all our plans in jeopardy.* The word comes from Old French *jeu parti*, divided game, originally an expression used to denote a problem in chess, then more generally an uncertain situation in any game in which the chances of winning or losing were even. From this sense developed, by the 14th century, the modern meaning of a risky situation from which harm or loss could possibly come.

Jerusalem artichoke

A *Jerusalem artichoke* does not have any connection with *Jerusalem*. The name is that of a kind of North American sunflower(*Helianthus tuberosus*) with tubers that are used as a vegetable. The name *Jerusalem artichoke* was an attempt to represent the Italian *girasole* ('sun-circler') *articiocco*, sunflower artichoke.

Job's comforter

A *Job's comforter* is a person who tries to sympathize with and encourage someone who is unhappy but who in reality makes him or her feel even more unhappy and distressed: *You're a real Job's comforter! I don't need you to tell me what a mess I'm in!* The expression relates to the Old Testament character of Job, whose so-called friends tried to 'console' him while telling him that his sorry state was largely due to his own disobedience to God. As Job said, Job 16:2: 'I have heard many such things: miserable comforters are ye all'.

jodhpurs

Jodhpurs are riding breeches that are wide at the hips but fit tightly from the knee to ankle. The name of the garment derives from *Jodhpur*, the former state, now a city in the state of Rajasthan in north-west India, where they were worn by riders. The breeches were introduced to England in the 19th century.

journal

A *journal* is a publication that is issued regularly – e.g. quarterly or monthly. According to its origin, however, it should be published every day. *Journal* comes from Middle French *journal*, daily, from Latin *diurnalis*, ultimately from Latin *dies*, day. Curiously, the French language has retained the strict meaning of the original, with *journal* remaining as French for 'newspaper'.

jump on the bandwagon

If someone is *jumping* or *climbing on the bandwagon*, he or she is taking part in an activity that others are already involved in and which is proving fashionable and successful. The expression derives from the time when American political campaigners publicized their cause by riding through a town on a horse-drawn wagon. In order to attract attention, a band played on the wagon – hence the term *bandwagon*. Local VIPs and other supporters climbed up on to the bandwagon in order to express their support, but sometimes for their own personal gain. And of course when one person jumped up on to the bandwagon, inevitably others would follow, to join the crowd, thinking that this was the fashionable thing to do. Nowadays the phrase is often used of people who support a cause when they can see that by so doing they will profit personally from the success of the venture.

K

ketchup

Ketchup (also spelt *catchup* or *catsup*) is a thick sauce made with vinegar and seasonings, particularly one made from tomatoes: *tomato ketchup*. The word came into English via Malay *kĕchap*, spiced fish-sauce, from Chinese (Amoy) *kōe-tsiap*, from *kōe*, seafood, and *tsiap*, sauce. It seems that the original condiment, which the Dutch imported in large quantities in the 18th century, may have been a sauce made up mainly of mushrooms that had been salted for preservation. Other words borrowed from Malay into English include: *bamboo*, *batik*, *kapok*, *orang-utan*, and *sago*.

kick the bucket

The expression *kick the bucket* is used in informal English to mean 'to die'. There are two explanations of the origin of this phrase. Some authorities suggest that when freshly slaughtered pigs were hung on a beam or frame (known as a *bucket*) at a market, they writhed around and would *kick the bucket*. Other authorities suggest that the bucket is the pail on which someone who intends to commit suicide stands on. The noose is then tied around the neck, the bucket is kicked away, and death inevitably follows.

kidnap

It may seem strange but the origin of the word *kidnap* was to *nap* (like the related word, *nab*, to steal) *kids*, children. The verb *kidnap* came from the noun *kidnapper*. The original (17th-century) kidnappers seized children in English towns and cities and sold them to be labourers and servants in the American plantations.

kill the fatted calf; kill the goose that laid the golden eggs

To *kill the fatted calf* is to give a great celebration in order to welcome someone, e.g. a returning member of one's own family. The expression derives from Jesus' parable as recorded in the Authorized (King James) Version of the Bible, Luke 15:23–24, to welcome home the lost ('prodigal') son: 'And bring hither the fatted calf, and kill it; and let us eat, and be merry: For this my son was dead, and is alive again; he was lost, and is found.'

To *kill the goose that laid the golden eggs* is to get rid of a source of valuable future income. The expression derives from an old fable in which a farmer owned a goose which laid eggs of gold. In his greed, the farmer decided to kill the goose, so obtaining all the eggs at once, rather than singly. But of course the dead goose could lay no more eggs.

knave

In old-fashioned usage, a *knave* is a dishonest man or a rogue, but in Old English the word (*cnafa*) was used simply to refer to a male servant or boy (compare modern German *Knabe*, boy), with no derogatory overtones. This sense is reflected with reference to playing-cards; the *knave* is the picture card with the lowest value, otherwise known as the *jack*. It was in the

13th century that the word gained the sense of 'dishonest man', just as servants who are badly treated may develop into mischievous youths.

knight

In the Middle Ages, a *knight* was a nobleman who served his lord or sovereign as a mounted soldier: *a knight in shining armour*. In modern times, a *knight* is a man who has been given a non-hereditary rank in recognition of his achievements or services, knights being entitled to use the title *Sir* before their name. Originally, however, the Old English word for *knight* (*cniht*) was used to refer to a youth or servant. It was during the age of chivalry when the position of servant to a lord or nobleman became prestigious that the word acquired its more positive sense. Interestingly, modern German has retained the sense 'servant' for the related word *Knecht*.

knock into a cocked hat

To *knock something into a cocked hat* means to beat something; to be much better than something: *The latest personal computer looks like knocking the competition into a cocked hat*. The origin of the expression probably lies in the game of skittles (ninepins) in which three skittles were set up in the form of a triangle, like a three-cornered cocked hat. When all the skittles apart from these three had been knocked down, the game could be said to have been *knocked into a cocked hat* – in other words, not to be of any real worth any more.

knuckle down; knuckle under

The *knuckles* are the pieces of bone on the finger-joints. But in the 14th century the word was used to refer to other joints, which may well give us the clue to the origin of these phrases. In to *knuckle down*, to start applying oneself seriously to work or study, the reference may be to the bones of the spine. So to *knuckle down* was literally to 'put one's back into the task'. A more picturesque explanation alludes to the game of marbles. Here to *knuckle down* was to put one's knuckles on the ground in an attempt to direct one's aim more accurately.

To *knuckle under* is to submit to someone; to admit defeat. The reference here is to the joints of the knees being referred to as *knuckles*. A sign of submission to one's master or conqueror was to go down on one's knees, hence to *knuckle under*.

kowtow

To *kowtow* to someone is to behave with humble respect towards someone, especially in an attempt to gain something from that person. The word comes from Chinese (Mandarin) *kòu*, to strike, and *tóu*, head. Originally, this respect was shown by going down on one's knees before a superior and touching the ground with one's forehead. Other words from Chinese that have been taken into English include: *kaolin, silk, soya, tea,* and *typhoon*.

L

lackadaisical

Someone who is *lackadaisical* lacks vitality or enthusiasm and is rather dreamy. The word comes from the archaic exclamation *lackaday*, which in turn derives from *alack the day*, used to show regret and dismay. If one is sorry about one's situation, the result is often a loss of enthusiasm and energy.

laconic

If someone is *laconic*, he or she uses very few words to express something. The word derives from *Laconia*, the ancient Greek district of which Sparta was the capital. Residents of Laconia were known for their austerity (their *Spartan* lifestyle) and also for their terse and pithy speech and writing. Perhaps the most famous instance of laconic style is seen in the reply given by the Spartan leaders to the threat made by Philip II, King of Macedon. His announcement is said to have been, 'If I enter Laconia, I will raze it to the ground'. The answer the Spartan magistrates gave was simply, 'If.'

a lame duck

Someone or something that is referred to as *a lame duck* is ineffective and unsuccessful and cannot exist or function without others' help. For example, an industry that is in financial difficulties and can only keep going with government assistance may be described as a *lame duck*. In the USA up to the 1930s a congressman who was defeated in the November re-elections remained in office up to the following March. They served the balance of their term in office as *lame ducks*, retaining some power and able to cause trouble if they so wished.

The origin of the expression may lie in the London Stock Exchange, where the term was used to describe someone who had been crippled financially – had lost all his or her money on the Stock Exchange and so was unable to pay the debts that were due. An alternative explanation is the old American hunting maxim, 'Never waste powder on a dead duck'.

lampoon

A *lampoon* is a spoken or written attack on someone or something that ridicules them in a strong satirical manner. The word dates back to the 17th century and comes from French *lampon*, probably from *lampons*, let us drink. This was part of the chorus of a drinking song.

landlubber

A *landlubber* is someone who does not enjoy travelling aboard ship or someone who is unfamiliar with life at sea. The word is not an alteration of *land lover*, as is popularly thought, rather, it is simply a joining of *land* and *lubber*, the latter word meaning someone who is clumsy or awkward. So a *landlubber*, according to the word's original meaning, was a stumbling novice – one who was completely inexperienced in the art of seamanship.

laser

A *laser* is a device that generates a beam of high-intensity light or other form of electromagnetic radiation. It has many uses, e.g. cutting hard substances, in holograms, in telecommunications, and in surgery. The word is an example of an acronym – a word made up of initial letters of other words. *Laser* originally stands for *l*ightwave *a*mplification by *s*timulated *e*mission of *r*adiation. Other scientific expressions that are cumbersome to say in full and so have been formed into acronyms include: *AIDS* from *a*cquired *i*mmune *d*eficiency *s*yndrome, *radar* from *r*adio *d*etecting *a*nd *r*anging, and *sonar* from *s*ound *n*avigation *r*anging.

laurel (look to one's laurels; rest on one's laurels)

The *laurel* in the expressions *look to one's laurels* and *rest on one's laurels* originally described the wreaths of this shrub with which the Greeks awarded poets, and victors at the Pythian Games. The Romans gave similar awards to citizens for outstanding achievements. So to *rest on one's laurels* is to feel so satisfied with the fame and distinction that one has already gained that one does not bother to try to achieve any more: *Now is not the time to rest on your laurels!* The idiomatic expression *look to one's laurels* means to maintain one's position, ensuring that others do not do better than one. See also *poet laureate* at POET.

leap year

A *leap year* is a year with 366 days, when February has 29 days instead of 28. This is to make up for the fact that a year in the Gregorian calendar (365 days) is in reality approximately one-quarter of a day shorter than the solar (or astronomical) year

(365.242 days), so that every four years the year has to have 366 days instead of 365.

The origin of the term *leap year* lies in the fact that while in non-leap years the days of the week move forward by just one day, in leap years they *leap* two days in months from March onwards. So, if 1 June is a Monday, it would be a Tuesday the next (non-leap) year. But if the following year is a leap year, it would be a Wednesday instead.

For years of the century (1800, 1900, etc.), the year must be divisible by 400. So the first centennial leap year since 1600 is 2000.

leave in the lurch; leave no stone unturned

If one *leaves someone in the lurch*, one deserts someone while he or she is in a difficult or dangerous situation. The meaning of *lurch* comes from Middle French *lourche*, an old dicing game that resembled backgammon. The word was also used to describe a player who was facing a decisive defeat in such a game. The player had no hope of winning – hence was in a helpless unsupported position.

To *leave no stone unturned* is to use every possible means to do something. The expression is said to originate as the advice of the oracle at Delphi to the Theban general Polycrates in 477 BC. Polycrates was searching for treasures that the defeated Persian general Mardonius was supposed to have hidden on the battlefield after the battle of Plataea (479 BC). The Delphic oracle advised him to move everything, which Polycrates did ... and he eventually found the treasure.

leotard

A *leotard* is a one-piece close-fitting garment worn by acrobats, ballet dancers, and others performing physical exercises. The garment is named after the French acrobat Jules *Léotard* (1842–70), who designed the costume and introduced it to the circus. Léotard was one of France's most well-known acrobats, starring in circuses in Paris and London. He perfected the first aerial somersault and invented the flying trapeze; he was known as 'That Daring Young Man on the Flying Trapeze'.

leprechaun

A *leprechaun* is a mischievous elf in Irish folklore, sometimes represented as a cobbler and traditionally believed to disclose the hiding place of a crock of gold if caught, and if his captor keeps his eyes on him. The word *leprechaun* comes from Irish Gaelic *leipreachān*, from Middle Irish *lúchorpān*, from *lū*, small and *corpān*, body. Other words from Irish Gaelic include: *brogue, galore, shamrock* and *smithereens*.

the letter of the law

The expression *the letter of the law* is used to refer to the literal strict understanding of the law. It is often used in contrast with the phrase *the spirit of the law*, the general purpose of the law: *To abide by the absolute letter of the law is just not possible all the time in life.* The expression derives from the Authorized (King James) Version of the Bible, 2 Corinthians 3:5–6: 'Not that we are sufficient of ourselves to think any thing as of ourselves; but our sufficiency is of God; Who also hath made us able ministers of the new testament; not of the letter, but of the spirit: for the letter killeth, but the spirit giveth life.'

lewd

Something that is obscene or suggests sex in a crude coarse way is sometimes described as *lewd*. This word derives from

Old English *ǣwede*, originally meaning 'lay; not belong to the clergy'. In the course of time, the word developed increasingly negative senses from 'lay', through 'ignorant; uneducated' to 'unprincipled; wicked', and finally to 'obscene; lascivious'. This is the only sense that survives in modern English.

libel

Libel is a false statement that damages someone's reputation and is published in a book or newspaper. The word comes from Latin *libellus*, little book. In Roman times and in early English use, if people wanted to defame someone, they would issue a small book full of attacks on that person's actions and character.

The terms *libel* and *slander* are sometimes confused. Both refer to defamatory statements, *libel* to written statements, *slander* to spoken statements. A handy way of remembering the difference is to link *libel* and *library* (associated with the written word) and *slander* and *slang* (associated with the spoken word).

lick into shape; a lick and a promise

To *lick something or someone into shape* is to improve something or someone by putting them into a proper presentable form: *A few weeks' hard discipline will certainly lick the new trainees into shape*. This idiomatic phrase comes from the old belief that a bear cub is born as a shapeless mass of flesh and fur and that its parents take turns to literally lick the cub into shape.

The expression *a lick and a promise* is used to describe a task that is done quickly and superficially. The phrase referred originally to the action of a cat briefly licking its paw and then quickly and lightly passing the paw over its face, with the supposed promise of a more thorough wash later.

limelight

The *limelight* is the centre of public attention; *For years he's been in the limelight*; *Once you've been on television a few times, it's difficult to stay out of the limelight*. The *lime* in the word is not connected with the colour of the lime tree, but is the chemical substance is heated it gives off a brilliant white light. This fact substance is heated it gave off a brilliant white light. This fact inspired the Scottish engineer and inventor Thomas Drummond (1797–1840) to create a device in which lime was heated in an oxy-hydrogen flame. Such devices formed part of the equipment that came to be used in lighthouses. After Drummond's death, limelight was used to illuminate theatrical stages. So the performer in the limelight was literally in the powerful beam of a spotlight and received the full glare of public interest and attention – hence the figurative meaning of the expression *in the limelight*.

limerick

A *limerick* is a humorous verse of five lines. The word derives from the name *Limerick*, a city and county of Eire, but the connection between the place-name and the verse form is uncertain.

Limericks were first composed in the 1820s, and were popularized by Edward Lear in his *Book of Nonsense* (1845). Strangely, these poems were not known as limericks originally. They were first called *learics*, and it wasn't until later in the century that the word limerick was used to describe these verses. It is probable that the name caught on because it comes in the chorus 'Will you come up to Limerick?' sung between the recitation of such nonsense verses at lively parties.

limousine

A *limousine* is a large luxurious car, especially one with a glass partition between the chauffeur and the passengers. The word comes from French, in which language it refers to a cloak or hood, particularly the hooded cloaks traditionally worn in the old French province of *Limousin*. The name came to refer to the car probably because the passenger compartment of such cars was likened to the hooded cloak.

lion's share

The *lion's share* is the largest part of something that is divided amongst several people, etc.: *The railways have traditionally had the lion's share of the market for transporting coal.* The expression derives from one of Aesop's fables. In the story, the lion goes hunting accompanied by other animals. When the spoils are shared out, the lion claims three parts out of the four: one part because he is the king of the beasts, one part because he is the strongest, one part because he is the bravest, and in the words he says to the other animals, 'as for the remaining part, touch it if you dare'.

a little learning is a dangerous thing

The saying *A little learning is a dangerous thing* means that to have just partial knowledge of something can result in more serious mistakes than not knowing anything in the first place. Pride should not lead people to think they know more than they actually do. The expression comes from Alexander Pope's *An Essay on Criticism* (1711):

A little learning is a dang'rous thing;
Drink deep, or taste not the Pierian spring.

lock, stock, and barrel

The expression *lock, stock and barrel* means everything: *When they emigrated, they sold all they had, lock, stock and barrel.* The expression is an old reference to the language of firearms. The *lock* is the mechanism that ignites the charge of a gun; the *stock* is the part of gun into which the barrel and lock are set, and the *barrel* is the tube through which the bullet is fired. So the *lock, stock and barrel* of a firearm is the whole gun.

loggerheads (at loggerheads)

Two people or groups who are *at loggerheads* are involved in a disagreement or quarrel. The original loggerheads were long-handled implements that had iron bulbs or balls on the end and were used to melt tar. During medieval times they were used in maritime battles: tar and pitch were heated up in the loggerheads and thrown at the enemy ships. The two sides engaged in the battle were thus said to be *at loggerheads* with each other.

long in the tooth

The expression *long in the tooth* means getting rather old: *He's getting a bit long in the tooth to be playing squash every evening!* The phrase was originally applied to horses' teeth. As horses grow older, their gums recede and it appears that their teeth get longer. Other expressions concerning horses' teeth are *don't look a gift horse in the mouth* (see under GIFT and *straight from the horse's mouth* (see STRAIGHT).

loo

A *loo* is an informal word, used especially in British English, for toilet. There are several explanations of the origin of this word. The two most likely are these. First, that the word is a British attempt to pronounce French *le lieu*, the place. (The *lieu* in the expression *to have time off in lieu* is often pronounced as *loo*.) The second is that it is a shortened version of *Gardy loo!*, the exclamation uttered by housewives as a warning when – in the days before sewers – chamber pots were emptied out of the windows into the street. *Gardy loo!* is a version of French *gardez l'eau*, watch out for the water!

loophole

Nowadays, a *loophole* is a way of escaping or evading something, especially an ambiguity or inexact wording in a contract or other document. The original loopholes take us back to medieval times. In medieval castles, loopholes are narrow windows that widen inwardly, but which are only tiny slits as viewed from the outside. Archers behind the windows were therefore able to direct their missiles easily, whereas opposing archers found these targets very difficult to aim at. The word *loophole* also referred to a similar opening that allowed air and light in or afforded a means of observation and from these senses developed the sense of an outlet or narrow means of escape.

love (love; love me, love my dog)

Love is a score of nil in tennis matches: *Thirty–love*. This term probably derives from the idea of *playing for money or playing for love* – i.e. playing with the aim of winning money or playing for *nothing* – without stakes, simply because one enjoys it.

The phrase *love me, love my dog* means that real affection and respect for someone should take in everything – particularly the less agreeable things – about that person. The saying is a very old one; it first appeared in Latin in the writings of St Bernard (1091–1153), abbot of the monastery of Clairvaux: *Qui me amat, amat et canem meum*, Who loves me will also love my dog. This St Bernard, incidentally, is not St Bernard of Menthon (923–1008), after whom the alpine passes and the breed of dog are named.

lunatic

The word *lunatic*, meaning insane, reveals something of ancient beliefs. The word derives ultimately from Latin *luna*, moon, since it was believed that madness fluctuated with the different phases of the moon. Lunatics were thought to become more and more frenzied as the moon increased to its full. A similar idea can be seen in the word *moonstruck*, meaning affected as if by the moon, e.g. mentally deranged.

M

mad (as mad as a hatter; as mad as a March hare)

The two similes *as mad as a hatter* and *as mad as a March hare* are used to refer to strange behaviour, eccentric or irresponsible actions, and madness. The Mad Hatter was a popular character in Lewis Carroll's *Alice's Adventures in Wonderland* (1865), but the phrase is much older than that. The expression may originally have been *mad as an atter*, *atter* meaning 'poison' being related to *adder*, the poisonous snake whose bite was formerly considered to cause insanity. Other authorities hold that the origin of the expression lies in the hat trade. Constant inhaling of the mercury that was used in making felt hats caused an uncontrollable twitching of the muscles that was regarded by some as a sign of madness. This explanation seems less likely than the first, however, as the expression was current before hat-making became an accepted trade.

The simile *as mad as a March hare* also has various explanations. Some authorities point to the supposedly more unpredictable and playful behaviour of hares in the mating month of March; others think that March hare is an alteration of *marsh hare*, a hare that is reputed to behave oddly because of the damp surroundings in which it lives. The March hare is also, of course, a famous character in *Alice's Adventures in Wonderland*.

madrigal

A *madrigal* is an unaccompanied song for several voices singing several different melodies. The word originally referred to a short love poem, especially one that could be set to music and came into English from Italian *madrigale*, which in turn derived from Medieval Latin *matricale*, simple or primitive. This came from Late Latin *matricalis*, of the womb, referring to a poem or song that was sung in the mother tongue.

maelstrom

A *maelstrom*, a very strong whirlpool, derives from the *Maelstrom*, the name given to the strong tidal current in the waters in the Lofoten Islands off the north-west coast of Norway. *Maelstrom* comes from Dutch *malen*, to grind and *stroom*, stream. Legend has it that two magic millstones aboard a ship sailing in this area ground out such a great quantity of salt that the ship sank. The millstones still went on grinding away underwater, however, which is why the waters in that area are so turbulent and salty. Originally used to describe this Norwegian whirlpool, the word passed into more general application, and is also used figuratively to refer to a confused, destructive state of turmoil.

magazine

A *magazine* is a weekly or monthly publication for a particular specialized readership: women's magazines; magazines for railway enthusiasts. The word, deriving ultimately from Arabic *makhzan*, storehouse, came into English in the 16th century to refer to a place where arms, ammunition, etc., were stored. It later came to stand for a storehouse of information, rather like our modern encyclopedia; with the advent of *The Gentleman's Magazine*, founded by the British printer Edward

Cave (1691–1754) in 1731, it came to refer to a periodical published for general readers. The first issue declared its aim to promote 'a Monthly Collection to treasure up, as in a Magazine, the most remarkable Pieces on the Subjects above-mention'd'.

magenta

The colour *magenta* is a deep purplish-red. The word came into the language in the second half of the 19th century, after the discovery of the dye from which magenta is produced. The dye was named after *Magenta*, a town in north-west Italy, near Milan, with reference to the notoriously bloody battle of Magenta in 1859, when the Austrians were defeated by French and Sardinian troops during the struggle for Italian independence.

malaria

Malaria is a disease in which there are recurrent attacks of fever and chills. Nowadays it is known that malaria is transmitted by the bite of mosquitoes; before the association of disease and mosquito was made, it was believed to have a totally different cause. *Malaria* derives from Italian *mala aria*, bad air. It was thought that the disease was caused by the foul, unwholesome air which was characteristic of marshy areas. When the true nature of the cause of the disease was discovered in the late 1800s, the original name was retained.

manna

The food that was miraculously provided by God for Moses and the Israelites during their wanderings in the wilderness was known as *manna*. Speculation has long continued concerning the exact nature of this food; it may have been an exudation from the tamarisk tree. In fact, this speculation is seen in the origin of the word itself. The word *manna* derives from the people's question, 'What (Hebrew *mān*) is it?', the Israelites calling it *mān*. (Exodus 16:14–15,31) The word *manna* sometimes occurs in the expression *manna from heaven* to refer to an unexpected and welcome gift.

manner (*to the manner born*)

The phrase *to the manner born* means 'accustomed by birth or natural gift for a certain function or way of behaving'. The spelling of *manner* is to be noted; it is not *manor*, as might be thought – with the idea that the manor house is intended and the phrase means 'born to take up a high wealthy position'. The origin of the phrase is Shakespeare's *Hamlet* (Act 1, Scene iv), in which Hamlet is commenting on the king's habit of nocturnal revelling:

But to my mind – though I am native here,
And to the manner born – it is a custom
More honour'd in the breach than the observance.

manure

The noun *manure*, animal excrement that is used as a fertilizer, comes from a verb, which derives from Middle French *manouvrer*, to work by hand, (from Latin *manu operare*, to work by hand, the root from which English *manoeuvre* derives). The word came into English as the verb *manouren*, to till or cultivate. The meaning was extended to include putting animal excrement into the ground, when, so it seems, a euphemism was needed for dung.

marathon

A *marathon* is a long-distance race, especially one that is 26 miles and 385 yards (42.195 kilometres) long. The word comes from *Marathon*, the site in Greece where the Persians were defeated by the Greeks in 490 BC. So the story goes, a messenger ran the distance (26 miles) from *Marathon* to Athens with news of the victory, but promptly fell dead after delivering his message. An alternative explanation of the word derives from the remarkable feat of a man named Pheidippides, who ran the 150 miles from Athens to Sparta in two days in order to rally troops before the battle of Marathon.

It is not thought that races of the length of the current race were run in the classical Greek Olympic Games. One was introduced into the first modern Olympic Games (1896), when a commemorative race was run from Marathon.

The word marathon is also used in the extended sense of a contest of endurance (e.g. *a darts marathon*). Interestingly, the ending -*thon* is used in the word *telethon*, a very long television programme to raise money for charity, formed from the words *tele*vision and mara*thon*.

margarine

Margarine is a yellow substance that is made from vegetable oils, animal fats, and water, and is used like butter. The substance was made originally in France in the 19th century from animal fats, one of which was known as *margaric* acid, *margaric* deriving from Greek *margaron*, pearl, in allusion to the pearly lustre of the acid's crystals. The pronunciation of the beginning of the second syllable with a *g*-sound, as in the name *Margaret*, is now rarer than the pronunciation with a *j*-sound, as in *margin*, but follows more closely the origin of the word.

marmalade

The preserve known as *marmalade* is made from a citrus fruit, particularly oranges. The word comes from Portuguese *marmelada*, quince jam, quince being the fruit from which marmalade was originally made. The Portuguese term itself derives from Latin *melimelum*, sweet apple, from Greek *meli*, honey and *mēlon* apple: the honey apple was, it seems, a variety of apple grafted onto the quince.

Other words that have come into English from Portuguese include: *caste* and *molasses*.

maroon

To be *marooned* is to be abandoned in an isolated or desolate place, for example a desert island. The word *maroon* was the name that was originally used in the 17th century to refer to fugitive Negro slaves and their descendants who set up communities in the most inaccessible areas of the West Indies and Guiana. *Maroon* comes from American Spanish *cimarrón*, savage or living on mountain tops, from Spanish *cima*, summit.

marshal

Nowadays a *marshal* is an important officer or official in any of certain spheres such as the air force or army, the police (in the USA), or the organization of a public event. But the word has not always been associated with a high status. Like CONSTABLE, the word had humble beginnings. The original marshals were mere keepers of horses, the word *marshal* being related to Old High German *marahscalc*, farrier or groom, from *marah*, horse, and *scalc*, servant. The word then came to be used for an important functionary in a medieval royal household or court, originally a man in charge of the cavalry, and then, when the cavalry became important in warfare, the office of marshal meant command of a sovereign's military forces. So the duties of marshal gradually rose in dignity and status.

martyr

A *martyr* is someone who undergoes death or great suffering rather than give up a belief. The word comes ultimately from Greek *martys*, witness, and was originally used as a term of honour to describe the first Christians who accepted the punishment of death for refusing to abandon their faith.

masterpiece

A *masterpiece* is an impressive work of art or piece of workmanship: *a masterpiece of engineering*. The origin of the word is not 'masterly work' or 'task carried out by a master', as might be supposed. The word referred originally to a sample of work that was submitted to a medieval guild as evidence that the craftsman who had undertaken it was qualified to have the rank of master in the guild.

Maundy Thursday

Maundy Thursday is the name given to the Thursday before Easter, to commemorate Christ's Last Supper with his disciples. The name *Maundy Thursday* comes from Old French *mandé*, something commanded, from Latin *mandatum*, commandment, from the Latin for Christ's words in John 13:34: *Mandatum novum do vobis*, 'A new commandment I give unto you'. This new commandment was 'that ye love one another; as I have loved you', and had been shown by Jesus' washing of his disciples' feet.

Tradition has it that on Maundy Thursday the reigning British monarch presents specially minted coins to a number of elderly people (one man and one woman for each year of her life) in a specially chosen cathedral city. Originally the monarch washed the feet of a few chosen poor before distributing food and clothes, but this practice stopped and gifts of produce were replaced by money.

mealy-mouthed

Someone who is *mealy-mouthed* is reluctant to speak openly and directly, particularly out of a desire not to offend people. The word may come from Greek *meli muthos*, honey speech, i.e. sweet insincere talk. An alternative explanation is that the origin lies in *mealy* in the sense 'soft-spoken', from *meal*, powdered grain. The *Oxford Dictionary of English Etymology* cites the second explanation, adding that it is 'perhaps based on a foreign idiom such as German *Mehl im Maule behalten*,' to carry meal in the mouth, i.e. to be indirect in one's speech.

meander

A river that *meanders* follows a winding course. The word was used originally to refer to the notoriously winding river in Asia Minor, known in Greek as *Maiandros* (now *Menderes* in south-west Turkey). The word came into English in the 16th century, via Latin *maeander*. The river is about 390 kilometres (240 miles) in length and flows south-west then west into the Aegean Sea.

meat

The Old English word for *meat* referred to all food, not just the flesh of animals used as food. This earlier meaning is seen for example in the Authorized (King James) Version of the Bible, Genesis 1:30: 'To every beast of the earth, and to every fowl of the air, and to every thing that creepeth upon the earth, wherein there is life, I have given every green herb for meat.' Since the 17th century, the word's meaning has narrowed to refer solely to animals' flesh. The former meaning of the word is preserved in the phrase *meat and drink* and also in the word *sweetmeat* (a delicacy made from or preserved in sugar).

meet one's Waterloo

The expression to *meet one's Waterloo* means to suffer a decisive defeat. The phrase alludes of course to Napoleon's final defeat by British, Dutch, Belgian, and German forces under Wellington and Prussian forces commanded by Blücher at Waterloo near Brussels in Belgium on 18 June 1815. Wellington's and Blücher's troops were separated; Napoleon tried to attack Wellington's forces directly, but they stood their ground until the Prussians came back into the battle and the French were routed. Four days later Napoleon abdicated.

melodrama

A *melodrama* is a play or film in an emotional or sensational style – but the original melodramas were somewhat different, as the origin of the word shows. *Melodrama* comes from the Greek *melos*, song, and French *drame*, drama. So the first melodramas were more like operas – romantic extravagant theatrical performances with sensational plots, music and songs. The name *melodrama* was retained after the songs and music were no longer part of the genre.

mercurial

Someone who is *mercurial* is likely to suddenly and unpredictably change his or her mind. The adjective derives from the name *Mercury*, the Roman god of commerce, travel, eloquence, etc., after which the planet Mercury is also named and the heavy silver-coloured liquid metal mercury. The meaning of the adjective *mercurial* reflects the sense of the metal which flows quickly from place to place and the ancient astrologers' belief that those born under the influence of the planet Mercury were prone to have quickly shifting changes of mood.

mesmerize

If someone is *mesmerized* by something he or she is extremely fascinated, spellbound, or even hypnotized by it. The word comes from the name of the Austrian physician and hypnotist Franz Anton *Mesmer* (1734–1815), who induced a hypnotic state in his patients. Born in Austria, Mesmer studied and later practised medicine in Vienna. He considered his medical success was due to his method of stroking his patients with magnets.

In spite of the support of those he had treated, Mesmer was compelled by the Austrian authorities to leave Vienna, so he moved to Paris in 1778. Here, his healing technique became very fashionable.

In 1784 Louis XVI appointed a scientific commission to investigate the practices; they concluded that Mesmer was a charlatan and an impostor. This led him to flee from Paris and he spent the rest of his life in obscurity in Switzerland. Mesmer believed that his success was due to the supernatural; today it would be recognized that it was due to his hypnotic powers.

mews

A *mews* is a small street or courtyard surrounded by buildings that were once used as stables. The word entered the language in the 14th century as the name of the royal stables built on the site of royal hawk-houses at Charing Cross in London – a *mew* being a room or cage in which hawks were kept especially when moulting, from Old French *muer*, to moult, ultimately from Latin *mutare*, to change. By extension, *mews* became the name given to any line of stables with living quarters above them.

midwife

A *midwife* is a nurse, usually a woman, who is trained to help women in childbirth. One widely-held explanation of the origin of this word is that the midwife acts as a *middle* person between mother and baby – a kind of 'go-between'. The word does in fact however derive from Old English *mid*, with (compare German *mit*), and *wif*, woman. So according to the word's origin, a midwife is someone who stays with a woman during the birth of her child, to assist her and to deliver the baby.

milliner

A *milliner* is someone who makes or sells women's hats. The word entered the language in the 16th century as *Milaner*, a trader in fancy goods from the Italian city of *Milan*. In the 16th century, Milan was famous as a centre of fashion and elegance, and was particularly well known for its bonnets, gloves, lace, and ribbons. In the course of time, the spelling of the word *Milaner* became specifically associated with the making and selling of hats.

mind one's ps and qs

The advice to someone, especially a young person, to *mind his or her ps and qs* is a warning to him or her to be very careful, especially not to say or do anything wrong. There are several explanations of the origin of this phrase. The most likely theory is that the phrase alludes to the difficulty that these letters present to a child who when learning to write must differentiate between a *p* and a *q*. A related explanation is that the phrase refers to the difficulty that an apprentice printer had in distinguishing between the two letters when selecting type. A third, more unusual suggestion concerns the chalking

150

up of a drinker's bill on a blackboard in a pub – *p*s for pints and *q*s for quarts. The publicans clearly had to make sure that they chalked up the *p*s and *q*s accurately when noting the quantities of drink consumed.

miniature

The word *miniature*, meaning small-scale, does not derive from *minimum* or *mini* as may be popularly thought. The word came into the language in the 16th century, via Italian, from Latin *minium*, red lead (vermilion). From this noun came *miniare*, to colour with red lead, the original *miniatures* being manuscripts containing letters which were illuminated with this red pigment. It seems that the word *miniature* was then wrongly applied to small portraits, because it was confused with Latin *minor*, smaller, and so came to refer to anything very small.

minion

A *minion* is someone who does an unimportant job or is a servile assistant or underling. The word has not always had such derogatory connotations, however. *Minion* comes from Middle French *mignon*, darling or loved one, which in turn came from *mignot*, dainty or delicately small. The original *minions* in English were favourites or dependants, serving their noble or monarch. From this sense developed the meaning of fawning servile attendant.

mint

The place where money is coined is known as a *mint*. The word comes from the Latin word for money, *moneta*. The ancient Romans coined their money in the temple of the

Roman goddess Juno, who was known by the title *Moneta*, the Admonisher. Thus it was that the mint and the coins made in it were known by this name.

minutes

Minute, one sixtieth of an hour and *minutes*, the official record of a meeting, both derive from the same Latin word, *minutus*, small. From this Latin word also came the verb *minute*, to record the proceedings of a meeting in tiny handwriting. This record was to be written up subsequently in large letters in a fuller version, a process known as *engrossing*. So while the original minutes of meetings were small hand-written transcriptions, nowadays they are records of meetings regardless of the size of the writing or printing.

mob

A *mob* is a disorderly or violent crowd of people. The word entered the language in the 17th century as the Latin phrase *mobile vulgus*, fickle or excitable crowd. This became shortened to *mobile*, and then abbreviated again to *mob*. This shortening enraged language purists, such as the British essayist and dramatist Sir Richard Steele (1672–1729), who wrote in his periodical *The Tatler*, 'I have done my utmost for some years past to stop the progress of "mob" ... but have been plainly borne down by numbers, and betrayed by those who promised to assist me.'

moment of truth

A *moment of truth* is a crucial time when one has to face up to an important reality and when everything is put to the test.

The expression comes from Spanish bull-fighting: the moment of truth (*el momento de la verdad*) is the point in a bull-fight when the matador plunges his sword into the bull to finally kill the animal.

moot

If a subject is *mooted* at a meeting it is raised for discussion. The word *moot* also occurs in the phrase a *moot point*, a matter on which there are different viewpoints that can be discussed but are not finally settled: *Whether they will accept our offer is a moot point.* The origin of *moot* lies in the Old English *mōt*, and *gemōt* a local English assembly that considered legal and administrative matters. The word is also seen in *moot* courts, mock courts in which law students practise their profession by arguing hypothetical cases, originated in the 16th century at the Inns of Court in London.

moron

The word *moron* is now chiefly used as an offensive way of referring to someone who is very stupid. Originally, however, the word had an exact scientific meaning. The word was suggested by the American psychologist Dr Henry H. Goddard (1866–1957) in 1910 at the American Association for the Study of the Feeble-Minded to designate a mentally deficient person with a mental age of between eight and twelve years old, with an intelligence quotient of between 50 and 70. The word derives from Greek *mōros*, foolish.

mountain (make a mountain out of a molehill)

The expression to *make a mountain out of a molehill* means that one makes something insignificant or trivial seem very important and serious. The sense of this idiomatic phrase was expressed by the 2nd century AD Greek satirical writer Lucian in his *Ode to a fly* in his phrase *to make an elephant of a fly*. It is this phrase in translation that remains a French and German proverb, but inexplicably this expression is not part of the English language in this form. The phrase *make a mountain out of a molehill* is first recorded in Foxe's *Book of Martyrs* (1570).

mulligatawny

The name of the rich meat soup known as *mulligatawny* does not derive from *mulligan stew* or the colour *tawny* as might be supposed, but is of Indian origin. The name comes from two Tamil words, *miḷaku*, pepper and *taṇṇi*, water. The name alludes to the spicy nature of the soup, which is flavoured with curry.

Other Tamil words that have come into English include: *catamaran*, *cheroot*, and *curry* itself.

mumbo jumbo

Mumbo jumbo is meaningless talk or gibberish. Originally, the word came from the Mandingo language, spoken in west Africa. *Mama Dyumbo* is said to have been the name of a tribal god or spirit who protected the local villages from evil spirits. It seems that the deity was at times impersonated by a man in order to punish offending women of the local village and to keep them in subjection. *Mumbo jumbo* is a changed version of the name of the deity and since the 'god' confused and bewildered the women, the word has come to refer to meaningless talk or nonsense.

muscle

A *muscle* is a tissue of elongated cells in an animal body that expand and contract to produce movement. The origin of this word is surprising ... the word came into English in the 16th century via Middle French from Latin *musculus*, little mouse. It seems that some muscles were thought to look like mice, or more humorously, the flexing of muscles were thought to resemble a small mouse moving about under the skin.

N

nail (on the nail; nail one's colours to the mast)

To pay cash *on the nail* is to pay money immediately. The expression referred originally to the medieval custom of market traders setting up a bollard-like structure (*nail*) in front of their stalls. Purchasers put their money on this short pillar and their change was placed on this also. The action of putting *cash on the nail* meant that the business deal was conducted promptly, justly, and openly — hence the figurative meaning of the phrase.

If one *nails one's colours to the mast*, then one states one's position on a matter very clearly and is determined not to change one's mind. The colour referred originally to the flag, generally national, on a warship. If a crew were prepared to surrender, the flag was taken down. If however the colours were nailed to the mast, they could not easily be removed. In other words, the crew were openly demonstrating their unwavering allegiance and their firm intention not to surrender.

navvy

A *navvy* is a labourer, a person whose job is to do hard physical work, e.g. building roads. The word is a changed shortened form of *navigator*, originally the name of a labourer in the 18th century who was concerned with digging of a *navigation*, an artificial inland waterway or canal. The arduous nature of such excavation is reflected in the phrase *to work like a navvy* meaning 'to work extremely hard at physical labour'.

neighbour

A *neighbour* is someone who lives near or next to another person. The word comes from Old English *nēah*, near, and *gebūr*, dweller. These two elements have come down to us as *nigh* and *boor* – which is what a neighbour was originally – a nearby rustic or farmer. The word *boor* has degenerated in meaning to refer to a person who is clumsy, ill-mannered, or rude. Its original sense is reflected in German *Bauer*, peasant or farmer, and in the word *Boer*, the first Dutch or Huguenot settlers, who were farmers, in South Africa.

nepotism

Nepotism is favouritism that is shown to relatives or close friends, especially by giving them jobs. The word comes via Italian from Latin *nepos*, nephew or grandson. The word was originally used to describe the popes' practice of granting special favours to 'nephews' (often a euphemism for illegitimate sons) or other members of the family. Perhaps the most notorious example of nepotism is seen in the actions of Pope Alexander VI (Rodrigo Borgia, c.1431–1503), who had his illegitimate son Cesare Borgia (c.1476–1507) installed as a cardinal when the boy was only 17 years old, granted his nephew Giovanni a cardinal's hat, and gave other members of his family similar special church offices.

nest egg

A *nest egg* is a sum of money that is saved up for the future. The term originally referred in the 17th century to an egg made of china or porcelain that a farmer put in a hen's nest to encourage the hen to lay more eggs. In the same way the setting aside of money is thought to induce the addition of further sums in order to accumulate even greater savings.

never-never land

Never-never land is an imaginary place where everything is ideal. The phrase was popularized by J.M. Barrie in his children's play *Peter Pan* (1904). *Never-never land* (or *country*) originally meant the remote northern part of Queensland in Australia. Those who visited this region promised, so it is said, 'never never' to come back.

new (*turn over a new leaf*)

If someone decides to *turn over a new leaf*, he or she is promising to start improving in behaviour: *He said he was going to turn over a new leaf when he came out of jail and he's not been in trouble with the police since.* The expression, which dates back about 500 years, does not, as might be supposed, allude to the leaf of a tree, but does refer to the leaves (sheets of paper) of a book. The phrase alludes to the turning to a blank page in an exercise book where one can start one's work anew. Figuratively, such a fresh start gives the possibility of learning a new lesson in the book of life's principles: a chance to begin again and mend one's ways.

news

News is (the broadcast report of) information about interesting or noteworthy recent events. The word does not, as is sometimes supposed, come from the abbreviations of the points of the compass, N, E, W, and S, as if it were reports coming from all 'corners' of the world. The word's origin is in fact much simpler: in Middle English the spelling was *newes*, modelled on Old French *noveles* or Medieval Latin *nova*, new things. It seems that the idea that the word is derived from the first letters of the points of the compass may have come from the practice of some newspapers printing a picture of a globe with the compass points N, E, W, and S on their masthead.

nice

Not many words in the language have changed their meaning as much as the word *nice*. In modern English the word is used in the sense of 'good or pleasant' to express general approval. The word goes back to latin *nescius*, ignorant, and came into the English language in the 13th century with the meaning 'foolish'. The senses developed in the course of time: in the 14th century 'wanton or lascivious', in the 15th century 'shy' and in the 16th century 'fastidious' or 'showing a fine distinction', a sense that is retained in such current phrases as *a nice distinction* and *a nice point*. It was in the 18th century that the word took on its principal modern sense.

nick (in the nick of time)

If something happens *in the nick of time*, it happens successfully but only just in time. A *nick* is a tiny cut, a notch, and the phrase *the nick of time* goes back to the former practice of keeping accounts and scores by cutting notches on a stick of wood known as a tally. See also TALLY. In a competition, the tally would be cut with a tiny groove on every occasion that one side scored. If one side scored right at the last moment and so won the game, then that particular nick was known as the *nick in time*.

nightmare

A *nightmare* is a very frightening dream. The word comes from *night* and -*mare*, but this second part of the word has nothing to do with a female horse, as if the dreamer were being carried off on a frightening ride by a wild mare. No, the *mare* comes from an obsolete Old English word *mare*, a demon or incubus that was thought to lie on one's body during sleep, causing a sense of suffocation during a bad dream. In medieval times, this evil spirit was known as a *night-hag* or *nightmare*, and by the 16th century the latter word was used to refer to a very distressing dream.

a nine days' wonder

A *nine days' wonder* is something that has a great appeal for a short time and is then forgotten. The origin of the phrase is said to lie in the fact that kittens and puppies are blind for the first nine days of their lives. During this time they live in a wonderful and mysterious world of their own. After about nine days everything becomes visible ... and more unexciting and ordinary: *the nine days' wonder* is over and done with for ever.

noisome

Noisome is one of those words that many people cannot quite remember the meaning of. It has nothing to do with noise. It is a formal word that means offensive and very unpleasant:

noisome fumes. The word comes from Middle English *noy*, annoyance – compare our modern *annoy* – and the suffix *-some*.

nose (on the nose)

The expression *on the nose*, meaning 'exactly; at target point' is said to have originated in the early days of radio broadcasting. Directors in soundproof control rooms made certain signals to their assistants performing the actual programme. Putting the forefinger alongside the nose meant that the programme was running precisely on time. Other signs included the director 'sawing' his throat forcefully to mean 'cut'.

O

oaf

An *oaf* is a foolish clumsy person. The word comes from Old Norse *alfr*, (elf), a changeling, a child supposedly left by fairies in place of a child that they had stolen. The spelling of the word became *oaf*, and its application became wider to describe an abnormal child. In the course of time, its meaning developed further and the word *oaf* is now used to refer to a clumsy idiot.

OK

The origin of the word *OK*, which is used to express general approval, has been widely discussed. There are two main theories of the word's origin. Some authorities suggest that it stands for *oll korrect*, a facetious re-spelling of *all correct*, coined in 1938. Other authorities believe that the source of the word is in the pair of initials *O*ld *K*inderhook, the birthplace in New York and later nickname of the Democrat Martin Van Buren, (1782–1862), who was seeking re-election as US President in 1840. The *O.K.* Club was formed to support his campaign. He was not re-elected, so the result was certainly not OK.

Whatever its origins, the word is firmly entrenched in English (with its variant spelling *okay*) and also other languages. Indeed, as Stuart Flexner writes in *I Hear America Talking*, 'OK is the most popular typical American expression. Short, slangy, and affirmative, this abbreviation is used millions of times a day in America, while foreigners around the world identify Americans by it – and use it themselves.' See also *A-OK* at A-1.

ombudsman

An *ombudsman* is an official who is appointed to investigate the complaints of individuals against public or government organizations. The word *ombudsman* comes from Swedish, in which language it means 'commissioner' or 'representative', the post originating in Sweden in 1809.

Tungsten (the heavy metallic element) is one of the few other words that has come from Swedish into the English language, from Swedish *tung*, heavy, and *sten*, stone.

onomatopoeia

Onomatopoeia is the forming of words that suggest or imitate the thing or action they represent. Examples of onomatopoeia are the words *buzz*, *crash*, *hiss*, *moo*, and *sizzle*. Poetry that echoes the sound of its subject is also onomatopoeic. A well-known example is Edgar Allan Poe's *The Bells*:

Keeping time, time, time,
In a sort of Runic rhyme,
To the tintinnabulation that so musically wells
From the bells, bells, bells, bells.

The word *onomatopoeia* itself comes from Greek *onoma*, name, and *poiein*, to make.

orgy

An *orgy* is a wild promiscuous party, or in an extended sense a wildly uncontrolled activity: *an orgy of destruction*. The original orgies were secret ceremonial rites honouring ancient Greek deities such as Dionysus and Demeter with drinking, singing, and dancing.

ostracize

If someone is *ostracized*, he or she is banished from a group or ignored socially. The word derives from Greek *ostrakon*, shell, tile, or potsherd. When the citizens of ancient Athens decided that a person should be removed because his power was considered too great for the freedom of the State, they wrote on a potsherd or tile the name of the person they proposed to banish. If 6000 voted in favour of a person's banishment, the victim had to leave Athens for ten years, although he did not forfeit his property. Not more than ten citizens were ever ostracized in this way and the practice ceased by the end of the 5th century BC.

ozone

Ozone is a form of oxygen with a chlorine-like odour that is used as a bleach; the *ozone layer* is a layer of ozone in the earth's stratosphere that helps to protect the earth from harmful ultraviolet rays from the sun. Although in informal use *ozone* is sometimes used to mean pure fresh air, e.g. at the seaside, the word comes from Greek *ozōn*, from *ozein*, to smell or stink. The name *ozone* was originally given to the gas 'because of its strong smell' by the German chemist Christian Friedrich Schonbein (1799–1868) in 1840.

P

Pacific Ocean

The *Pacific Ocean*, the world's largest ocean was named by the Portuguese explorer Ferdinand Magellan (c.1480–1521). After travelling through the stormy strait that was to be named after him between the mainland of South America and the archipelago of Tierra del Fuego, Magellan found the ocean so comparatively calm that he named it the *Pacific*, from Latin *pacificus*, peaceful. Magellan led the Spanish expedition that was the first to circumnavigate the world. He himself was killed in the Philippines, with only one of the expedition's original five ships, the *Victoria*, under Juan Sebastián del Cano (c.1460–1526), returning to Spain in 1522.

paddle one's own canoe

The word *canoe* goes back to the days of Columbus and comes from Haitian *canoa*, originally a small boat hollowed out from a tree trunk. The expression *paddle one's own canoe* means to be independent, to make one's own decisions, to be self-sufficient. The phrase goes back to the early 19th century and was popularized by Abraham Lincoln who frequently used the phrase. It is also recorded in the novel *The Settlers in Canada* (1844) by the English novelist and naval officer Frederick ('Captain') Marryat (1792–1848): 'I think that it much better that as we all go along together, that every man paddle his own canoe.'

pagan

Someone who does not follow one of the main religions of the world is sometimes described as a *pagan*. The word derives from Latin *paganus*, countryman or villager. The word *paganus* was also used by Roman soldiers to refer disparagingly to a civilian. Since the early Christians thought of themselves as members of Christ's army, they used the derogatory military term *paganus* to refer to someone who was not 'a soldier of Christ'.

paint the town red

To *paint the town red* is to have a lively enjoyable time in places of public entertainment, especially to drink a lot of alcohol: *The day the exams finished they decided to really paint the town red.* The expression goes back to the 19th century and may originally have alluded to a town's red-light district with its brothels and saloons. So a party of wild cowboys in carefree pursuit of a night's entertainment could well want to paint the whole town red.

pale (beyond the pale)

If something is *beyond the pale*, it is not socially acceptable: *His remarks about the royalty were completely beyond the pale.* The *pale* in this expression has nothing to do with the whitish colour but comes originally from Latin *palus*, pole or stake. Since stakes are used to mark boundaries, a pale was a particular area within certain limits. The *Pale* from which the expression *beyond the pale* comes was the area around Dublin in Ireland, in which English law operated in medieval times until the 16th century. Those who lived *beyond the pale* were outside English jurisdiction and were thought to be uncivilized.

palindrome

A *palindrome* is a word, phrase or sentence that reads the same backwards as forwards. The word derives from Greek *palindromos*, running back again, from *palin*, back or again, and *dramein*, to run, the earliest palindromes being devised by the ancient Greeks. Examples of palindromes in English are: *Hannah*, *level*, *minim*, and (the longest palindromic word in English) *redivider*; the remark attributed to Napoleon, *Able was I ere I saw Elba*; and the 19th-century couplet:

> Dog as a devil deified
> Deified lived as a god.

The longest palindromic story has 66,666 words and was composed by Edward Berbow (1987). It begins 'Al, sign it, "Lover!"' and so ends, 'revolting, Isla'.

pallbearer

A *pallbearer* is someone who helps carry the coffin. The *pall* in this word comes from Latin *pallium*, a covering worn by men in ancient Rome that was made by draping a rectangular cloth around the body. At funerals such a cloth was used as a covering for the coffin of only distinguished men, with the original pallbearers each holding a corner of the pall as they carried the coffin. Today a pallbearer is a person who helps carry the coffin (whether or not it has a pall), and also someone who walks as part of the escort of the coffin at a funeral.

pamphlet

The ending – *let* often means 'small', e.g. *booklet*, *droplet*, so it could be thought that *pamphlet* (an unbound printed publication with a paper cover) was a similar word. This is not the case, however. The word *pamphlet* comes from the name of a 12th-century Latin love poem '*Pamphilus seu De Amore*', (Pamphilus or On Love), Pamphilus being a masculine proper name. This short Latin love poem evidently became so popular that it came to be known simply as *Pamphilet*, later *pamflet*, and eventually *pamphlet*. The sense of a brief treatise on a matter of current interest was added in the 16th century.

pan out

The verb *pan out* means 'to turn out; develop or succeed': *We'll see how things pan out*. The word derives from the language of gold mining. Prospectors would wash earth in a shallow pan by running water through it in the hope of finding traces of gold. When gold was not found, the miners would say that it hadn't *panned out*. From the language of gold prospecting, the expression was used to refer to plays or books that failed – that hadn't *panned out* – and then into general usage.

pandemonium

Pandemonium is a state of chaos or wild uproar. The word was coined by the English poet John Milton in Book 1 of *Paradise Lost* (1667). Milton used the word as a name for the capital of hell where all the evil spirits met for their council: 'A solemn Council forthwith to be held At Pandæmonium, the high Capital of Satan and his Peers'. The word derives from Greek *pan-* all, and *daimōn*, spirit.

pansy

A *pansy* is a small garden plant with velvety petals of white, yellow, or purple. The word comes from Middle French *pensée*, thought, from *penser*, to think, since at one time it was supposed that the plant with its petals resembled a thoughtful face. The plant was known as a *pensee* in the 15th century, but in the course of time its spelling and pronunciation were changed to give our present *pansy*. The word has also been used since about the first quarter of the 20th century to describe a man who is weak and effeminate or a male homosexual.

pantechnicon

A *pantechnicon* is a very large lorry that is used for moving household furniture from one place to another. The word derives originally from Greek *pan-*, all, and *technikon*, of the arts, and was originally the name of a building in Motcomb Street, near Belgrave Square in London that was established to sell Victorian works of art. Unfortunately the venture was a commercial failure and the building became used as a furniture storage warehouse. The name, however, survived and was used to describe the vehicles that were used in furniture removal to and from the former arts centre.

pantomime

The original *pantomime* was completely silent theatre with one masked actor playing many parts, the word *pantomime* coming via Latin from Greek *pan-*, all, and *mimos*, imitator. English pantomime originally consisted of action without speech but in the 18th and 19th centuries, under the influence of the harlequinade and burlesque, developed into the dramatized traditional fairy-tale performed at Christmas with popular songs, dances and topical comedy. Traditionally, the role of principal boy is played by a woman and that of the comic old woman (dame) is played by a man.

paraphernalia

The word *paraphernalia* is nowadays used to refer to a large number of miscellaneous things: *He collected together all his books, his typewriter and other paraphernalia and loaded them into the car.* The word comes from Greek *parapherna* and was originally used to refer to the goods that a bride brought to her marriage that were over and above (Greek *para*, beside) the dowry (Greek *phernē*, dowry). Thus, the paraphernalia of a married woman were the items that she was legally entitled to regard as her own.

parchment

Parchment is the skin of an animal, especially a sheep or goat, that was formerly used as a material for writing on, or paper made to resemble this. The word comes ultimately from *Pergamon* (Pergamum), the ancient city of Asia Minor (now the site of Bergama in Turkey) famous for its library and where parchment was first developed in the 2nd century BC. It seems that parchment was first developed at Pergamum because Ptolemy refused to supply papyrus, the alternative writing material, from Egypt. The paper was known as *pergamena charta*, paper of Pergamum, which became French *parchemin*, probably influenced by Latin *Parthica pellis*, literally '*Parthian leather*', a kind of scarlet dyed leather.

parlour

The present-day sitting room was formerly known as a *parlour*. The word *parlour* derives from Old French *parleur* and was originally a reception-room that was set aside for conversation in a convent or monastery. It then came to be applied to a small room in a mansion, dwelling house, town hall, etc., e.g. *the Mayor's parlour*. The original meaning of *parlour* has now all but vanished, and the word is used in such expressions as *a funeral parlour* or an *ice-cream parlour*, when it refers to a place for conducting any of various kinds of business.

a parting shot

A *parting shot* is a hostile comment that is made at the end of a conversation when leaving, so allowing its recipient no opportunity to give an answer to it. The expression was originally a *Parthian shot* and alludes to the practice of the ancient archers of Parthia (of south-west Asia) who were renowned for shooting arrows at their enemy pursuers while fleeing ... or pretending to flee.

pay through the nose

To *pay through the nose* is to have to pay an excessive price for something: *Why pay through the nose for expensive kitchen refitting when you can use our economical reliable service?* There are various theories regarding the origin of this expression. Some authorities suggest that the derivation lies in *rhino*, slang for money. Since *rhinos* is Greek for 'nose', the expression may have evolved from the similarity of *rhino* and *rhinos*. A second theory is that the expression originated with the idea of being 'bled' for money – from *nosebleed*. A third theory is that the expression derived from a poll tax levied upon the Irish by the Danes in the 9th century. Those who failed to pay the tax were unfortunate enough to have their noses cut off.

pecking order

The *pecking order* amongst people in a group is a graded order of hierarchy or seniority: *Small companies remain at the bottom of the pecking order when it comes to receiving payment from an insolvent company.* The expression referred originally to the natural order that exists in a flock of birds, e.g. domestic fowl. Each bird pecks those lower in the scale without fear of retaliation. So within a human pecking order, everybody knows his or her place – the position indicated by how much he or she is dominated by people of higher rank and by how much he or she dominates those of lower rank.

pedigree

The *pedigree* of an animal is the record of its ancestry, especially when the line of ancestry is a distinguished one. The word *pedigree* comes from the language of genealogy. The three-lined symbol used by genealogists in the Middle Ages when drawing lines of succession on family trees was thought by some to resemble the bony foot of a crane, or as Middle French had it, a *pie de grue* (*pie*, foot; *de*, of; *gru*, crane). This came to stand for not only the symbol but also the ancestral line and the genealogy itself. The word entered English in the 15th century and the spelling gradually changed to give the current form *pedigree*.

peg (*take someone down a peg or two*)

To *take* or *bring someone down a peg or two* is to make someone who is self-important and conceited have a more humble opinion of himself or herself. The expression probably originally referred to a ship's flags. These were raised or lowered by pegs – the higher the position of the flags, the greater the honour. So to *take someone down a peg or two* came to mean to lower the esteem in which that person is held.

penguin

A *penguin* is a flightless sea-bird with short legs that is found in Antarctic regions. The name of this bird is believed to come from the Welsh *pen gwyn*, white head, from *pen*, head, and *gwyn*, white. It is said that this name was originally applied by Welsh sailors not to the penguin but to the great auk (*Pinguinus impennis*), a flightless diving bird once common in the North Atlantic but extinct since the mid-19th century. When explorers in southern territories saw a bird that resembled the great auk, they used the same name for it. Given the word's origin, however, this name is inaccurate since a feature of the penguin is that its head is black.

perk

A *perk* is an incidental benefit or privilege that is in addition to one's normal salary. Examples of perks include a company car, private health insurance, and special financial help with mortgages. This word does not have the same origin as *perk up*, to liven up, as might be supposed, but is a shorter and changed form of *perquisite*, originally (in the 15th century) possessions of property acquired by means other than by inheritance. The word *perquisite* later came to be used to refer to casual profits and then to a tip or gratuity. In current English *perquisite* is the term used for *perk* in very formal contexts.

person

The word *person* (an individual human being) comes from the Latin *persona*. This was the term used in Greek and Roman drama to refer to the mask worn by an actor to play a particular part. (For example, a pale mask with sunken cheeks and flowing light hair represented an unwell young man.) The word *persona* came to stand for the player acting the part, the character portrayed and eventually to a human being. The Latin word *persona* is still retained in the phrase *dramatis personae*, a list of the characters or actors in a play and in the word *persona*, the identity or 'image' that a person presents to others.

pickle (*in a pickle*)

If you are *in a pickle*, you are in a difficult and confused situation: *See what a pretty pickle you've got us into now!* The expression comes from the Dutch *in de pekel zitten*, to sit in the pickle, *pickle* being the brine used to preserve meat and vegetables. To be seated in such a salty liquid would indeed be uncomfortable.

pidgin

A *pidgin* is a simplified language that is made up of elements of two or more other languages and is used particularly for trade by people who speak different languages. The origin of the word *pidgin* itself is probably a Chinese mispronunciation of the English *business*. Originally, *pidgin English* was developed by British traders in China and consisted of English words and Chinese syntax.

A pidgin is not the mother tongue of any speech community, but when it becomes such a language, it is known as a *creole*. As David Crystal writes (*The Cambridge Encyclopedia of Language*, CUP), 'The term *creole* comes from Portuguese *crioulo*, and originally meant a person of European descent who had been born and brought up in a colonial territory. Later, it came to be applied to other people who were native to these areas, and then to the kind of language they spoke.'

pie in the sky

Pie in the sky is the promise or prospect of something pleasant in heaven or in the future – something that is unlikely to happen. The phrase comes from the song *The Preacher and the Slave* (1906) by the union organizer and songwriter Joe Hill (1879–1914):

> Work and pray (work and pray)
> Live on the hay (Live on hay)
> You'll get pie in the sky when you die.
> (That's a lie.)

The phrase is a parody of a hymn by Ira Sankey, 'The Sweet By and By'.

a pig in a poke

To buy *a pig in a poke* is to buy something without first examining what exactly one is purchasing. The expression goes back to the days of selling a cat instead of a suckling pig at a market. A con-man would approach possible buyers with a single piglet. This animal was, so it would be claimed, a sample of those that were tied up in bags (*pokes*) awaiting sale. The customer would pay up and then realize he had been tricked when, opening up the poke, he or she would literally let the cat out of the bag. See also *let the cat out of the bag* under CAT.

pillar (from pillar to post)

To go *from pillar to post* means to go from one place to another: *I spent hours at the County offices – they sent me from pillar to post trying to find the right department to deal with my query.* The origin of this expression goes back to the game of court tennis, rather like modern squash. The original phrase was *from post to pillar*, because the ball in a certain volley would strike first a post and then a pillar. As the expression came to be used in spheres outside the game, so the order of the nouns was reversed.

pin money

Pin money is a small amount of money, to be spent for example on things that one wants but does not really need: *They expect me to be a middle-aged married woman who works just for pin money.* Pin money was formerly an allowance of money given to wives for clothes and other personal expenses, and the expression may well have an earlier origin. Before pins were mass-produced in the 19th century, their manufacture was controlled by a monopoly granted by the British crown. They were therefore very expensive and so sums (*pin money*) were set aside specially to purchase them. It is said that at the beginning of each year wives would ask their husbands for pin money and then buy as many as they could at the market. If the price of pins decreased, the allowance was spent on other personal goods, and in this sense the phrase has lingered in the language.

piranha

A *piranha* is a ferocious freshwater fish found in tropical America. The effects of its strong jaws and razor-sharp teeth on its unfortunate victims will be familiar to devotees of James Bond films. The name of the fish is appropriate, as *piranha* comes via Portuguese from the South American language of Tupi, in which it means fish with teeth, from *pirá*, fish and *sainha*, tooth.

Other words from South American languages that have come into English include: *condor, jaguar, llama, pampas, poncho, tapioca* and *toucan*.

plain (as plain as a pikestaff)

If something is *as plain as a pikestaff*, it is very obvious or easy to recognize: *I don't know how you missed it! There were labels marked 'Fragile' on the packet, as plain as a pikestaff*. The *pikestaff* in this expression may well originally have been *packstaff*, the stick on which a traveller carried his or her pack over the shoulder. In time, such a staff would become worn – plain or smooth from regular use. Other authorities suggest that the reference is to a pike, a weapon formerly used by infantry, a spear with a metal spike on the end: the shaft of the spear (the *pikestaff*) was long and so clearly visible.

plain sailing

If something is *plain sailing*, it is easy and will progress without difficulty in a straightforward manner: *Once we've got this bolt back on, the rest of the job should be plain sailing*. The spelling of the phrase was originally *plane sailing* which was an expression used in navigation. Plane sailing is a simplified method of determining the position of the ship on the assumption that the earth is flat. A chart on a flat level surface was used, on which the lines of longitude and latitude were straight and parallel, so making no allowance for the curvature of the earth. In the 19th century the expression became used in non-technical contexts to refer to easy straightforward progress and the established spelling for the figurative use is now *plain sailing*.

poet laureate

The *poet laureate* is the poet who is appointed by the British monarch to be a lifetime officer of the royal household and to write poems for special occasions, e.g. a coronation or a state funeral. The first official appointment to poet laureate was of

John Dryden in 1668. The word *laureate* derives from Latin *laurus*, laurel, used with reference to a person who is specially honoured; compare also the expression *look to one's laurels* and *rest on one's laurels* under LAUREL.

But why should laurel be connected with honours in this way? The answer lies in ancient Greek mythology. According to the legend, the god Apollo was pursuing the nymph Daphne. Daphne begged the gods to help her and they immediately changed her into a laurel bush. This tree then became sacred to Apollo, who decreed that laurel should be the honour given to poets and victors.

polecat

The word *polecat* is used to refer to two animals – first a mammal of Africa, Europe, and Asia that is related to the weasel and gives off an unpleasant smell and second, in US usage, the skunk. The name *polecat* probably comes from a combination of Middle French *pol*, cock, and Middle English *cat*. The Middle French element is a changed form of *poule*, chicken. The animal was so named since it was thought to resemble a cat that preyed on poultry.

pooh-pooh

If someone *pooh-poohs* something, he or she expresses contempt for it: *For years people have pooh-poohed the idea of a tunnel under the English Channel and yet here it is becoming a reality.* The phrase goes back a long time. It is first recorded as *puh* by Shakespeare (*Hamlet*, Act 1, Scene iii: 'Affection, puh! You speake like a greene Girle.') In the 17th-century the word was doubled to give *pooh-pooh*, doubtless to express even greater dismissiveness.

posh

Something that is *posh* is smart and grand in appearance: *a posh new car*. There are two main explanations of the word's origin. The first, more picturesque explanation takes us back to the times when British passenger ships sailed regularly to and from India, in the days when India was part of the British Empire. In order to avoid the direct glare of the sun, some passengers wanted to be accommodated in rooms that were on the shaded side of the ship on both the outward and homeward journeys. This, so it is said, became known as travelling *p*ort *o*ut, *s*tarboard *h*ome, hence the acronym *posh*, with reference to the fashionable class of people who could afford the high price of the cabins. This explanation, although popular, has no evidence to support it. The second, less colourful, but more likely, explanation is that the word derives from the obsolete slang word *posh*, meaning 'dandy' or 'money', perhaps originally from Romany.

possum (play possum)

To *play possum* is to pretend to be asleep, dead, or ignorant in order to deceive someone. The expression alludes to the habit of the American *opossum* which pretends to be dead or unconscious in order to avoid being threatened or attacked by other animals.

The word *possum* comes from *opossum*, originally a thick-furred American marsupial with an elongated snout, from a Virginian Algonquian (American Indian) language, *oposon* or *opassom*, white animal. The word *opossum* is also used to refer to any of several Australian tree-dwelling marsupials.

Other words that have come into English from American Indian languages include: *moccasin*, *moose*, *papoose*, *POWWOW*, *raccoon*, *tepee* and *totem*.

179

pot (go to pot; the pot calling the kettle black)

If something has *gone to pot*, it has become worse or ruined. There are several different explanations of the origin of this expression. Some authorities suggest that it is inferior cuts of meat that are put into a pot for stewing. Other authorities suggest that it is a dead person's ashes that are put into an urn or pot. A third explanation is that the reference is to stolen items of silver or gold that were melted in a pot in order to avoid being identified or recovered in their original form.

The saying the *pot calling the kettle black* means that one is criticizing another person for a fault that one is guilty of oneself. The expression may have originated from the fact that both a pot and a kettle were black from standing so long on an open fire. Each was as black (hence, figuratively, bad) as the other. An alternative explanation is that the pot had a black surface while the kettle was shiny. On seeing its reflection in the kettle's polished surface, the pot asserted that the kettle, rather than it, was in reality black. No doubt the kettle replied angrily, 'Look who's talking – what about yourself!' The source of the phrase is probably Cervantes' *Don Quixote*, 'The pot calls the kettle black'.

potato

A *potato* is the name given to the round vegetable with a brown or red skin that grows underground. The word *potato* comes from *batata*, a word from the extinct Arawakan language of Taino, but it did not originally apply to what we now know as the potato. It was what we know as the *sweet potato* that the Spanish originally found in the West Indies in the 16th century. They adopted the word *batata* for this plant, in Spanish *patata*, and so *potato* in England. When the Spanish later found a different plant (the 'real' potato) in Peru, they thought it was simply a different variety of the West Indian tuber and so gave it the same name as the earlier plant.

one's pound of flesh

To demand *one's pound of flesh* is to insist on one's full legal right to something that is due to one, even though such a demand is unreasonable and may bring suffering to the person from whom it is due. The origin of the expression is Shakespeare's *The Merchant of Venice* (Act 4, Scene i), in which the moneylender Shylock tries to enforce an agreement that would permit him to remove a pound of flesh from the body of the merchant Antonio.

the powers that be

The powers that be are the controlling authorities, the government, or the Establishment: *I suppose the powers that be know what they're doing by cutting our research grant by a third.* The expression derives from the Authorized (King James) Version of the Bible, Romans 13:1: 'Let every soul be subject unto the higher powers. For there is no power but of God: the powers that be are ordained of God.'

powwow

In informal English a *powwow* is a meeting or discussion. The word derives from *powwow* in the Algonquian (American Indian) language, where it was used to refer to a medicine man or sorcerer. The first settlers used the word in the same way, but later applied it to the magical ceremony at which the medicine man performed. In due course the word came to refer to a meeting, conference, or discussion.

precarious

If something is *precarious*, it is hazardous or insecure: *seated precariously in a mountain cable car*; *in a precarious financial position*. The root of the word shows that a person who lives precariously would do well to depend on prayer: the word comes from Latin *precarius*, obtained by entreaty or prayer. The original source word is Latin *prex*, prayer.

precocious

A child who is *precocious* shows a much higher level of intelligence and development than other children of his or her own age. The word in this sense is an extension of the word's original meaning. *Precocious* comes from Latin *prae-*, before, and *coquere*, to ripen or cook. So precocious plants are those that ripen early or prematurely. This sense is still found in botanical usage.

prestige

If something has *prestige*, it has a high standing in the sight of others, because of its success, wealth, or status: *the prestige of working in the City of London*. The word originally had a quite different meaning, however. Its origin goes back via French to Latin *praestigiae*, conjuror's tricks (from *praestringere*, to bind tightly or blindfold). From this sense, developed the meaning of an illusion, and later, glamour achieved by success. The original meaning of the Latin source is retained in the formal or humorous word *prestidigitation*, sleight of hand or conjuring skill.

prevaricate

If someone *prevaricates*, he or she consciously avoids doing or saying something, as if to disguise the truth and so deceive others. The word came into the English language in the 16th century from Latin *praevaricari*, to walk crookedly. This word was originally used to refer to a bandy-legged person – one with crooked legs who couldn't walk in a straight line. The word was also used to describe a farm-worker who ploughed a crooked furrow. From these literal senses came the figurative application – a prosecutor in a court of law who made a secret arrangement with the opposite party and then went on to betray his own client. So developed the sense of one who deviates from stating the truth straightforwardly and gives 'crooked' answers.

proletariat

The *proletariat* is the working class; and in Marxist theory, the class of wage-earners in a capitalist society who depend solely on the sale of their labour to live. The origin of the term shows up a rather different background, however. The word comes from Latin *proles*, offspring. In ancient Rome the proletariat was the lowest class who served the State not by owning property but by having children.

propaganda

Propaganda is information, ideas etc., that is disseminated in order to sway opinions or sympathies. The word goes back to the *Congregatio de propaganda fide*, Congregation for propagating the Faith. This was the name of the committee set up by Pope Gregory XV in 1622 to direct the work of missions throughout the world. Originally referring to the dissemination of religious doctrine, the word *propaganda* came to refer to the spreading of political information and is now usually used in a pejorative sense.

protocol

Protocol is a code of correct or conventional procedures of behaviour at official or ceremonial occasions. The word comes from Late Greek *prōtokollon* (from *prōt*, first and *kollan*, to glue), which was a sheet glued to the front of a manuscript or the first sheet of a manuscript. This sheet bore details of the manuscript's manufacture or contents. The word's original reference to written material is seen in three meanings of the word that are less commonly in use today: first, the original draft of an agreement, especially one that forms the basis of a treaty; secondly, the summary of an agreement, for example one reached in international negotiations; and thirdly an amendment to a treaty.

punch

Punch is a drink made from alcoholic liquor, mixed with hot water, sugar, lemons, and spices, and served at parties. The origin of the word is traditionally thought to be Hindi *pãc*, five, from Sanskrit *pañca*, five: the drink is said to originally have been made of five ingredients: alcohol (wine or spirit), water or milk, sugar, spices, and lemon juice.

puny

A person or thing that is said to be *puny* is small and weak or feeble: *What a puny excuse!*; *puny little fingers*. The origin of the word is Middle French *puisné*, younger or born afterwards, from *puis*, afterwards, and *né*, born. The term originates from the belief that children born after the first child were weaker or more frail than the first-born. Interestingly, Middle French *puisné* from which puny derives, survives in English: *puisne* (pronounced in exactly the same way as *puny*) is a legal expression meaning 'lesser' or 'less important'. A *puisne* judge is a judge of lower rank.

pupil

The *pupil* of the eye is the opening in the centre of the iris. The word comes from Latin *pupilla*, little doll, little girl, or ward, from *pupa*, girl. The word came to be used to describe a part of the eye because of the very small image of oneself that can be seen reflected in the eye of another person.

Pupil in the sense of 'schoolchild' is a related word – it comes from *pupillus*, male ward, from *pupus*, boy or child, and *pupilla*.

python

A *python* is a large non-venomous snake that winds itself around its prey and then crushes it by constriction. The word derives from the name of the monstrous serpent *Pythōn* of Greek mythology. This dragon arose from the mud after the flood that Deucalion survived, and guarded Delphi. It was after killing Python that Apollo set up his oracle at Delphi.

Q

Quaker

A *Quaker* is a member of a Christian group that is known as the Society of Friends. Quakers are known for their emphasis on the 'Inner Light' (the divine presence that enlightens and guides), their rejection of sacraments and set forms of worship, their pacifist stance, and their promotion of causes of social reform. An early English Quaker, William Penn (1644–1718) founded Pennsylvania on a Quaker basis.

The name *Quaker* came from a statement uttered by George Fox (1624–91), the founder of the Society, in a court action in 1650. Fox, so it is said, urged the court's judge to 'quake and tremble at the word of the Lord'. The judge then contemptuously called him a *quaker*. Some authorities quote an earlier source (1647), with reference to a sect of foreign women that met at Southwark, 'called *Quakers*, and these swell, shiver, and shake'.

quarantine

Quarantine is the isolation that is imposed on people or animals for the sake of preventing the spread of a contagious disease: *Animals must be kept in approved quarantine premises for six months on entry to the United Kingdom, to avoid the dangers of rabies.* Different suspected diseases have different periods of isolation. According to the origin of the word, however, the period of quarantine should continue for 40 days. The word *quarantine* comes from the Italian *quarantina*, period of 40 days, which ultimately comes from the Latin *quadraginta*, 40. The word was applied originally to the period during which ships suspected of carrying people with a contagious disease were kept in isolation from the shore.

queue

If people stand in a *queue* or *queue up*, they are standing in a line, waiting for something, e.g. for a bus to come or to buy a ticket. This word, which is used mainly in British English, comes from the French *queue*, tail, which comes ultimately from the Latin *cauda*, tail.

quiche

A *quiche* is an open pastry shell with a savoury egg and cream or milk filling, e.g. of bacon or ham. The word comes from French, from the Alsatian (Lorraine) dialect version of German *Küche*, little cake, from German *Kuchen*, cake. *Quiche* was originally a speciality of Lorraine, a region of north-eastern France bordering on Germany.

quiz

A *quiz* is a game in which the knowledge of contestants is tested by a series of questions. The origin of this word is, however, uncertain. One interesting story of the word's origin takes us back to the Dublin of the 18th century. It is said that a theatre manager, James Daly, bet a friend that he could invent a new word and make it the talk of the town within 24 hours. As the story goes, Daly then got young people to chalk up the word *quiz* on every wall throughout the city. The next morning the word was obviously *the* topic of conversation – and so Daly won his wager and the language acquired a new word.

The word originally described first a hoax or practical joke – since that (if the story is true) is what Daly played on the people of Dublin, and secondly an eccentric person, again Daly, if ever there was one. In time *quiz* came to mean 'make fun of verbally' and gradually the sense developed of asking questions to find out how much someone knows.

R

rack (go to rack and ruin)

If something *goes to rack and ruin*, it falls to pieces, decays, or becomes very badly organized because it is neglected. The *rack* in this expression has no connection with the former instrument of torture, but comes from *wrack*, itself a variant spelling of *rack* in this phrase. This *wrack* means 'something destroyed' and comes from the Old English *wræc*, misery, persecution, or something driven along by the sea.

rain (rain cats and dogs; take a rain-check on something)

If it is *raining cats and dogs*, it is raining extremely heavily. There are two main theories of the origin of this expression. Some authorities suggest that the phrase goes back to the times of such poor drainage in cities that a severe rainstorm would easily cause many cats and dogs to be drowned. When the storm was over, many dead animals would lie around the streets — as if they had fallen, with the rain, from the sky. Other authorities suggest that the expression goes back to Norse mythology, in which dogs were associated with storms and the wind and cats with the rain.

To *take a rain-check on something* is an expression that is used mainly in American English and means to postpone acceptance of an offer. The *rain-check* in the expression was originally the stub of a ticket for an outdoor event. The stub was retained by a spectator who was allowed free admission to a later performance or replay of an event if it was interrupted by rain.

read the riot act

If you *read the riot act to someone*, you warn someone in very strong terms that he or she will be punished if he or she continues to behave badly: *After Dad came up and read the riot act to them, the twins soon quietened down and fell asleep.* The reference is to the Riot Act of 1715 (repealed in 1973). The manner in which this was used was as follows. If twelve or more people had gathered illegally, a magistrate could command them to disperse by reading the declaration of the opening of the Act: 'Our Sovereign Lord the King chargeth and commandeth all persons assembled immediately to disperse themselves and peacefully to depart to their habitations or to their lawful business.' Those who did not obey the order within an hour of this proclamation would be guilty of breaking the law.

reason (ours not to reason why)

The expression *ours not to reason why* is sometimes said when a superior issues an order that has to be obeyed without question when one does not understand why the order has to be carried out. The phrase is in fact a misquotation from the poem by Tennyson *The Charge of the Light Brigade* during the Crimean War:

Their's not to make reply,
Their's not to reason why,
Their's but to do and die:
Into the valley of Death
Rode the six hundred.

recipe

A *recipe* is a set of instructions with a list of ingredients to be used in the preparation and cooking of a particular dish. The word came into English in the 14th century from Latin *recipe*, meaning literally 'take!' This imperative form of the verb *recipere*, to take, was not originally part of cooking instructions, but was used as the first word in a medical prescription with the meaning 'take the following'. This medical application is still retained today, with the *recipe* indicated by an *R* with a slanting line / across the right-hand tail of the character.

red herring; red-letter day; red tape; like a red rag to a bull; see red

Originally, a *red herring* was a herring that had been pickled in such a way that its smell was very strong. It was used in hunting to draw the hounds away from the foxes' trail: the herring was dragged along the ground and left a much more powerful scent for the dogs to follow. In this way the dogs became confused, were thrown off the scent, and so would go in the wrong direction, following a false trail. Hence the present-day meaning of a *red herring*: something irrelevant, something designed to divert people's attention from the main subject being considered.

A *red-letter day* is a day that is looked forward to or remembered as being especially happy, important, or rewarding: *The day Norman and Mandy won the football pools was a real red-letter day!* The expression derives from the medieval practice of printing in red the religious festivals and saints' days on almanacs and calendars, while other days were printed in black.

Very bureaucratic procedures that seem unnecessary and cause delay are called *red tape*: *The government plans to reduce red tape to help set up new businesses.* The expression arose from the former use of a reddish tape to tie up bundles of official legal or governmental documents.

If something is described as being *like a red rag to a bull*, it will make someone violently angry. The allusion here is clearly to bull-fights and the traditional belief that the flourishing by a matador of a red cloth will be seen by the bull, who *sees red* – is roused to anger – and will attack. (Curiously, the popular belief that bulls dislike the colour red is probably wrong. It is the movement of the matador's cape, not its colour, that rouses the bull.)

rhinoceros

A *rhinoceros* is a massive mammal with a very thick skin and either one or two horns on its snout. The word *rhinoceros* entered the English language via Latin in the 13th century and derives from Greek *rhinokerōs*, from *rhis*, nose, and *keras*, horn, evidently from the daunting appearance of the huge horn(s) on the animal's head.

rickshaw

A *rickshaw* is a small two-wheeled vehicle that is used for carrying passengers. It is pulled by one or more people, and was originally used in Japan but is now found in other parts of Asia. The word *rickshaw* comes from Japanese *jinrikisha*; and this word can be divided up into its constituent parts: *jin*, man, and *riki*, power, and *sha*, carriage. So literally a rickshaw is a manpower vehicle.

Other words from Japanese that have become part of the English language include: *judo*, *karate*, and *kimono*.

ride roughshod

To *ride roughshod over someone or something* is to treat the person or thing harshly or insensitively: *The party leader's readiness to ride roughshod over a few dissenting party members*. The reference in this expression is to the practice by blacksmiths of leaving the heads of nails projecting slightly from a horse's shoe in order to give a better grip, e.g. on muddy or icy ground. Besides this, the shoes fitted to horses in battle sometimes had sharp protrusions, in order to inflict the greatest injury on those in their path. In each instance, the horse was described as being *roughshod*.

riding

Up to 1974, Yorkshire in England was divided into three *ridings*, or administrative divisions: North Riding, East Riding, and West Riding. The word *riding* does not derive, as may be thought, from its countryside being suitable for horse-riding, but in fact comes from Old English *thriding*, from Old Norse *thrithjungr*, a third part. In other words, each riding was originally a 'thirding', or one of three areas. The Danes who settled in this part of England considered Yorkshire to be too large an area to be administered as one unit, so divided it into three. The initial *th-* of the Old English word *thriding* became dropped by assimilation with the *t* or *th* of the part of the name that came in front of it: *west* th*riding*, *east* th*riding*, *north* th*riding* became *west riding*, etc. Although Yorkshire is no longer divided into ridings, the riding is still used as the name of an administrative or electoral area in parts of the Commonwealth such as Canada and New Zealand.

riff-raff

If a group of people are called *riff-raff*, they are being regarded as a worthless rabble. The word *riff-raff* came into English in the 15th century, from Middle French *rif et raf*, completely or one and all. Later, due to the influence possibly of French *rifler*, to plunder, and *raffe*, sweeping up, the sense became altered to refer to the rubbish, dregs, or 'scourings' of society.

rigmarole

A *rigmarole* is a long or complicated procedure: *We had to go through the whole rigmarole again just to register a change of date for the meeting*. The word *rigmarole* is an alteration of the term *Ragman Roll*, the name of an official roll of names of Scottish noblemen who paid homage to King Edward I in the late 13th century. The noblemen declared their loyalty to the King by signing individual deeds which were then joined together with many hanging seals into a rather confused and ragged-looking 40-foot-long document. *Ragman roll* was also the name of a list of characters in a medieval game, the list beginning with the name *Ragemon le bon*, Ragman the good. Players of the game each randomly drew out a verse on parchment by an attached string. The characters of the verses were unconnected and so the verses presented a confused and rambling series of statements or 'rigmarole'.

ring the changes

To *ring the changes* means to vary the choice that is made within a selection of things that are available: *After a month of eating at the same restaurant, Bob found he'd rung all the changes on the menu.* The expression derives from bell-ringing, or in particular, change-ringing, the art of ringing church bells in a set order that is constantly changed, a change being the order in which the set of bells is rung. It has been calculated that it would be possible to ring 479,001,600 changes with twelve church bells without repeating their order – a feat that, it is said, would take nearly 38 years. That is certainly ringing some changes!

rival

A *rival* is a person or group that is competing against another. The word comes via Middle French from Latin *rivalis*, literally 'one who uses the same stream as another', from Latin *rivus*, stream. Human nature being what it is, arguments would arise between one neighbour (*rivalis*) and another over the right to use the water in the stream – one wanting to use it for irrigation, the other for fishing or for his cattle. In this way, the word developed the sense of 'adversary or competitor'.

robot

The word *robot*, an automated machine that performs human tasks, comes from the Czech *robota*, work, or slave labour. The word came into the English language after being used as part of the title of a play by the Czech playwright and novelist Karel Čapek (1890–1938). The play was entitled *R.U.R.* (Rossum's Universal Robots) and was written in 1920, its first English performance being in London in 1923. In the play, the robots are artificial beings that perform mechanical tasks skilfully, but lifelessly.

The adjective *robotic*, of or like robots, was first coined by the US scientist and writer Isaac Asimov (1920–) in 1941.

room (*no room to swing a cat*)

The expression there's *no room to swing a cat* means that a particular space is very small, cramped, or crowded. The *cat* in this phrase may well be the *cat-o'-nine tails*, the whip used to flog disobedient sailors. Below deck, conditions were so cramped that there was *not enough room to swing a cat*, so the punishment was carried out on deck. Other authorities suggest that the *cat* was originally a sailor's hammock or cot.

roses all the way

The expression *roses all the way* is used to refer to a life of constant ease and pleasure. The phrase is commonly used in the negative: *Don't think that when you're married it'll be roses all the way*. The phrase derives originally from the poem *The Patriot* (1855) by the English poet Robert Browning (1812–89):

It was roses, roses all the way
With myrtle mixed in my path like mad.

rostrum

A *rostrum* is a platform for public speaking. The word is derived from Latin *rostrum*, bird's beak (which in turn comes from the Latin verb *rodere* to gnaw, the source of our word *rodent*). The word *rostrum* came to be used to describe the bow of a ship, since the bows were elaborately carved and so were thought to have the appearance of the beaks of giant birds.

When in 338 BC the Romans were victorious at Antium (now Anzio), they brought back the prows of some of the enemy ships to Rome. The ships' prows were then used to decorate the Forum in Rome and were used as platforms from which orators addressed the people, and hence our modern word *rostrum*.

round robin

A *round robin* is a written document that is circulated among the members of a group for their consideration. The *robin* in this phrase is not connected with the bird, as may be thought, but was originally French *ruban*, ribbon. The original French expression was *ruban rond*, round ribbon, and goes back to the France of the 17th or 18th century. At that time, government officials who wanted to petition the crown signed a ribbon that was arranged in circular form and attached to the document. In this way no one person could be held responsible for the document's contents. The custom was also used in the British navy: petitions of grievance bore a list of signatures that were arranged like the spokes of a wheel. Nowadays besides referring to a letter, a round robin is also a sporting tournament in which each contestant plays every other contestant in turn.

rub (there's the rub)

The expression *there's the rub* means 'that is what the difficulty is': *Ah! There's the rub – we all want to see new roads and factories built just as long as they're not in our own back yard*. The phrase comes from Shakespeare's *Hamlet* (Act 3, Scene i):

To die, to sleep;
To sleep: perhance to dream: ay, there's the rub;
For in that sleep of death what dreams may come
When we have shuffled off this mortal coil,
Must give us pause.

rule of thumb

A *rule of thumb* is a rough way of working, using one's experience and practical common sense rather than precise and accurate technical theory or knowledge: *A rule of thumb is that about one-third of its revenue comes into the shop in the two months before Christmas*. There are two theories of the origin of this expression. One is that a brewer formerly tested the temperature of a batch of brew by dipping a thumb into it. From the brewer's considerable experience, this *rule of thumb* would be sufficient to show him how the brewing was getting on. Or, more simply, the expression derives from the practice of using the last joint of the thumb as a rudimentary measure of approximately one inch.

rule the roost

If someone *rules the roost*, he or she controls others in a particular place. The reference in the expression is probably to the cock's showy dominance over his hens. There is also, however, a probable earlier version of the phrase, *rule the roast*. Here, the allusion is to the lord of the manor presiding over the carving of roast meat at table: the one who *ruled the roast* was certainly the master of the house.

S

sabotage

Sabotage is the deliberate destruction of machinery, railway lines, installations, etc., by enemy agents or protesting workers. The word came into English in the early 20th century and comes from French *sabot*, wooden shoe or boot. The first cases of sabotage were probably peasants who trampled a landowner's crops with their wooden shoes in order to gain higher wages and better working conditions. Alternatively, the first instances of sabotage may have been industrial workers throwing their wooden shoes into machines in order to render their factory inoperative. A third suggestion is that the original sabots were the shoes that fix railway lines to sleepers, and it was by removing the shoes in the French railway strike of 1912 that great disruption was caused.

sack (give someone/get the sack)

To *get or be given the sack* is to be dismissed from one's job by one's employer: *He got the sack for stealing the company's money.* This expression probably goes back to the time when a worker carried the tools of his trade in a sack or bag which he kept with his employer. In discharging him from his work, the boss would give the worker the sack, to be precise, the one in which the worker had brought his tools when he had taken on the job. The worker would then put his tools back into his bag and leave to look for work elsewhere.

sacrament

A *sacrament* is a Christian ceremony that is considered particularly important, for example baptism or communion. The word derives from Latin *sacramentum*, which was an oath of allegiance. At the beginning of a military campaign, Roman soldiers pledged their loyalty by taking such an oath. The word was also used in law-courts for the money deposited by the contestants of the legal action. Possibly owing to the formal characteristics of the ceremony involved with the *sacramentum*, the word became applied to Christian religious ceremonies. The Catechism of the *Book of Common Prayer* defines a sacrament as 'an outward and visible sign of an inward and spiritual grace given unto us, ordained by Christ himself'.

sacred cow

A *sacred cow* is something such as a belief, tradition, or organization that is considered with such great respect that it cannot be criticized in any way: *Some people think that the social sciences have become sacred cows in our modern world, never doubting or questioning their principles for a moment.* The expression alludes to the veneration of the cow by Hindus: the animal may not be killed for food.

salad days

The expression *salad days* is used to refer to a time of youth or inexperience. The phrase has its origins in Shakespeare's *Antony and Cleopatra* (Act 1, Scene V) and Cleopatra's words:

My salad days
When I was green in judgement, cold in blood.

The allusion is to the days of being 'green' – the time of naive, inexperienced and immature youth.

salary

A *salary* is the sum of money paid to an employee, usually paid monthly. The word *salary* comes from Latin *salarium*, a ration of salt (Latin *sal*) that was included as part of the wages given to Roman soldiers. The salt was used to preserve meat and to add flavour to food. In due course the method of payment became changed to an allowance of money for the purchase of salt and then payment for work undertaken, or 'salary'. The phrase *worth one's salt* alludes to the same origin. A worker who is worth his or her salt undertakes duties competently and so deserves a salary.

the salt of the earth

People who are described as being the *salt of the earth* are thought to have a fine, kind character and are regarded as being of great value. The expression comes from the words of Jesus in the Sermon on the Mount, as recorded in the Authorized (King James) Version of the Bible, Matthew 5:13–14: 'Ye are the salt of the earth: but if the salt have lost his savour, wherewith shall it be salted? it is thenceforth good for nothing, but to be cast out, and to be trodden under foot of men. Ye are the light of the world.'

salver

A *salver* is a decorated tray, usually made of silver, on which food or drinks are served, particularly on formal occasions. The word *salver* has no connection with *silver*, as might be supposed, but comes via French from the Spanish *salva*. A *salva* was a tray from which the food-taster of a king sampled food and drink in order to make sure that it had not been deliberately poisoned. The Spanish verb *salvar* meant 'to save' and 'to test in order to detect poison'.

sandwich

A *sandwich* is a snack consisting of two slices of buttered bread with a filling between them. The name derives from the English diplomat John Montagu, 4th Earl of *Sandwich* (1718–92). The Earl was addicted to gambling, some of his gambling sessions lasting as long as two days non-stop. He was so compulsive a gambler that, rather than leave the gaming table to take food, and so interrupting the game, he would order his valet to bring him food. Invariably, he would be brought food that consisted of slices of cold beef between two slices of bread. Within a few years the snack became generally known as a *sandwich*, although it had of course been eaten before this time.

sanguine

A person who is *sanguine* is confident and optimistic. The word derives from the Latin *sanguis*, blood. *Sanguine* originally meant 'having the colour of blood', or ruddy. Its contemporary meaning goes back to the days when four liquids or humours were thought to determine a person's disposition. (See COM-PLEXION). If a person had a ruddy complexion, this was considered to be due to the predominating influence of blood in the person's system, and hence, his or her character was cheerful and warm.

The original Latin word *sanguis*, blood, is also seen in the formal English word *sanguinary*, bloody, violent, or bloodthirsty.

sardonic

Sardonic laughter or behaviour is characterized by bitter or scornful derision. The word comes from the Greek *sardonios*, of Sardinia. This term was originally used to refer to a herb on the island of Sardinia that was allegedly so bitter that anyone who tasted it would have convulsions and grimaces of disdain. Victims of the herb's effects were also said to literally die laughing. The term *sardonic* is also reflected in the medical usage *risus sardonicus*, a strange grin caused by muscular spasm around the mouth, present in strychnine poisoning and tetanus.

scapegoat

A *scapegoat* is someone who is made to take the blame for the actions of others. The word was coined by the English Protestant William Tyndale (?1494–1536), from the words *escape* and *goat*, intended to translate the meaning of Hebrew *'azāzēl* (which was possibly the name of a demon) which was confused with *'ēz 'ōzēl*, the goat which escapes (Leviticus 16:8). The scapegoat was the goat that symbolically bore all the sins of Israel and was sent off into the wilderness.

scot-free

To get away from something *scot-free* means that one does not have to pay any penalty or suffer any loss or punishment: *Don't think you'll get off scot-free just because your Dad's a policeman!* The origin of the expression *scot-free* has nothing to do with Scots or Scotland, as may be thought, but dates back to the 13th century. A *scot* (from Old Norse *skot*) was then a municipal tax. Someone who went scot-free was exempt from paying this tax. The word *scot* was also later used to refer to the sum of money owed for entertainment, especially drinks, at a tavern: so someone who had a drink 'on the house' was also said to have gone scot-free. The sense gradually developed to apply to freedom from penalty, loss, or harm, not just from the payment of money.

scratch (come up to scratch)

A person or thing that *comes up to scratch* has reached an acceptable or satisfactory standard: *His performances as a violinist haven't really come up to scratch since his illness*. The phrase goes back to the days of prize-fighting, popular in the 18th and 19th centuries. The sport knew nothing of rounds of a set time, as with modern boxing, the rounds in those days continuing until one of the fighters was knocked down. A pause of 30 seconds then followed, after which each fighter had to reach a mark that had been scratched in the centre of the ring. The fighter who failed to 'come up to scratch' was regarded as being unable to fight any longer and so the other fighter was declared the winner.

sell someone down the river

If someone is *sold down the river*, he or she feels betrayed or cheated: *The workers feel they've been sold down the river by the union leaders who've accepted the management's pay offer*. The phrase dates back to the 1830s when American slaves were, as a punishment, sold to the owner of a sugar-cane plantation on the lower Mississippi, where conditions were the harshest. The expression *sell someone down the river* later came to be used to mean 'to take advantage of someone, for some personal gain'.

send someone to Coventry

If someone is *sent to Coventry*, he or she is ignored or ostracized. There are several different theories of the origin of this expression. The two most widely held are these. First, that in the English Civil War captured Royalist (Cavalier) prisoners were sent to Coventry, a strongly Roundhead (Parliamentary) town, where clearly they would be shunned. An alternative theory suggests an extreme dislike by the citizens of Coventry for soldiers in the city. The ordinary townspeople refused to associate with the soldiers, and women who did talk to the soldiers were OSTRACIZED.

serendipity

Serendipity is the art of making interesting discoveries by chance. The word was coined by the English writer Horace Walpole (1717–97) in 1754, based on the title of the Persian fairy-tale *The Three Princes of Serendip*. In the story, the heroes possessed this talent: 'they were always making discoveries, by accidents and sagacity, of things which they were not in quest of'. *Serendip* is the ancient name for Sri Lanka.

shambles

A *shambles* is a state of chaos or disorder: *We'd done no washing-up or cleaning while Mum and Dad were away, so the whole house looked a right shambles.* The word *shambles* comes from Old English *scamul,* stool or counter. In medieval times, the word was used to refer to a table or stall on which a butcher displayed his meat at a market. (The currency of the street name *The Shambles,* e.g. in York, goes back to the days when a whole street consisted of a row of butchers' stalls.) The word then came to refer to the place for slaughtering animals. An obvious feature of such a scene was chaotic confusion – hence the modern meaning of the word.

shanks's pony

To go by *shanks's pony* is a humorous way of saying 'to walk'. The phrase, which dates back to the 18th century, alludes to the *shank,* the part of the leg between the knee and the ankle, the plural of the noun *shank* being humorously used as a family name. The US equivalent of *shanks's pony* is *shanks's mare*.

shibboleth

A *shibboleth* is a belief, custom, or saying, particularly one that distinguishes members of a certain group or is no longer considered important. The origin of the word lies in the biblical story as recorded in Judges 12:4–6. In a battle between the Gileadites and the Ephraimites, the former group captured the fords of the Jordan. When the Ephraimites wanted to cross the river, they were asked if they were Ephraimites. If they replied in the negative, they would be asked to say the word *shibboleth* (Hebrew 'stream') as a test of their true identity, since the Gileadites knew that Ephraimites could not pronounce the 'sh' sound correctly. Those who pronounced this word wrongly were killed.

Other words from Hebrew that have become part of the English language include: *amen, jubilee, kibbutz* and *kosher*.

ship (*like ships that pass in the night*)

The phrase *like ships that pass in the night* is sometimes used to describe two people who meet each other briefly and then never see each other again. The expression derives from the poem *Tales of a Wayside Inn – The Theologian's Tale – Elizabeth*, by the US poet H.W. Longfellow (1807–82):

Ships that pass in the night, and speak to each other in passing;
Only a signal shown and a distant voice in the darkness;
So on the ocean of life we pass and speak one another,
Only a look and a voice; then darkness again and a silence.

206

shipshape and Bristol fashion

The expression (*all*) *shipshape and Bristol fashion* is used to refer to something that is tidy, neat, and organized efficiently. The phrase goes back to the time when Bristol, England, was an important trading port for sailing-ships. For long risky voyages the ships and their equipment obviously had to be in perfect order and Bristol had a reputation as a port for efficiency of the highest order.

short (*give someone short shrift*)

To *give someone short shrift* means that one treats him or her in an impatient and abrupt manner: *The politician gave his hecklers short shrift when they interrupted him.* Originally, the phrase was used to refer to someone who was about to be executed in public. To give that person *short shrift* was to grant him or her a brief time to make a confession of sins and to receive absolution before being executed.

A word related to *shrift*, confession, is seen in *Shrove* Tuesday, the day immediately before Ash Wednesday (the first day of Lent), from the verb *shrive*, to confess and to grant absolution.

show a leg

If one says, '*Show a leg!*' to someone, one wants him or her to get out of bed as quickly as possible. The expression is said to go back to the time when women were allowed on board ship when the ship was in port. In the morning, the women were allowed to lie in. The call to *show a leg* by the bo'sun's mate meant that the occupant of a hammock had to identify himself or herself by showing his or her leg. If a woman's leg emerged, she could go back to sleep. If a man's leg was shown, he had to get up and carry out his duties.

silhouette

A *silhouette* is the outline of a dark shape set on a light background. The word takes its name from the French politician Étienne de *Silhouette* (1709–67), but the precise reason for this is uncertain. As Controller of Finances (1759), Silhouette had to restore the French economy after the Seven Years War. He therefore instituted a series of stringent tax revisions, which made him unpopular. His measures were seen as niggardly and the phrase *à la silhouette* meaning 'on the cheap' became current. The sense of parsimony was then applied to the partial shadow portraits that were fashionable at that time.

Other authorities suggest that the brevity of Silhouette's period of office as Controller-General – he was forced to resign after only nine months – is the origin of the incompleteness of the portraits.

Still others claim that Silhouette's hobby was in fact making such outlines and he is said to have displayed many examples of this art form in his château.

silly

A person or thing that is *silly* is foolish, but the word has not always been used as an expression of disapproval. In fact, the opposite was originally the case. The probable origin of the word is the Old English *sælig*, happy or blessed (compare modern German *selig*). The sense of the word gradually changed from this to 'innocent', 'simple', and 'unworldly', 'feeble' with the meaning gradually acquiring more and more negative values, to reach its present meaning of 'foolish or showing a lack of good sense'.

sinecure

A *sinecure* is a job that is paid but involves little work. The word was originally a 17th-century ecclesiastical term and referred to a church office that yielded an income but had no responsibility for pastoral matters, or 'cure of souls', which is what the word originally means: *sine*, without, and *cura*, care or cure (of souls).

sinister

Something that threatens or suggests harm or evil is sometimes described as *sinister*. The word derives from Latin *sinister*, on the left side or unlucky, the two meanings going together. This was the sense followed by Greek augurs, that inauspicious omens appeared on the left side of a soothsayer who faced north and auspicious omens appeared on the right. (Roman augurs faced southwards and so the omens were reversed: see AUSPICES.)

The word *sinister* is one example of the language appearing to discriminate against left-handed people. *Gauche*, awkward, from French, 'left', has derogatory connotations, while *dexterous*, skilful, from Latin *dexter*, on the right side and *adroit*, skilful, from French *à*, to, and *droit*, right, have positive overtones.

sirloin

A *sirloin* is a cut of beef from the upper part of the hind loin. The word comes from Middle French *surlonge*, from *sur*, over, and *longe*, loin. The change in spelling from *sur* to *sir* is popularly thought to have come about in the following way. A British monarch, variously thought to be Henry VIII, James I, or Charles II, very impressed with the quality of a cut of beef, is said to have invested it with a knighthood, uttering the words, 'Arise *Sir Loin*.'

This story is said to be the basis of the calling of a double sirloin that is joined at the backbone a *baron* of beef, as a baron takes precedence over a 'Sir'.

six (*at sixes and sevens*)

To be *at sixes and sevens* is to be confused or disorganized: *We're all at sixes and sevens this morning, this new timetable's not working out at all well.* The phrase is an old one; it is found in Chaucer, and is said to have originated in a game of dice in which players tried to throw a six and a seven (perhaps originally a five and a six). To roll such numbers was recognized as being difficult. So it was only players who were determined, hence perhaps confused and disorganized, who would attempt such a throw.

skin (*by the skin of one's teeth*)

If one does something *by the skin of one's teeth*, one only just manages to do it: *They escaped death by the skin of their teeth.* This idiomatic expression derives from the Authorized (King James) Version of the Bible, Job 19:20: 'My bone cleaveth to my skin and to my flesh, and I am escaped with the skin of my teeth.'

slapstick

Slapstick comedy is comedy in which the performers behave in a silly rough manner, play simple practical jokes on each other, etc. The name of this kind of comedy derives from a more literal use of the noun *slapstick*. This was originally an apparatus made of two flat pieces of wood hinged at one end. The two pieces of wood would slap together noisily when used by one performer to strike a blow at other performers.

slipshod

Slipshod, meaning careless or slovenly, was originally used in the 16th century to describe people who walked around *shod* in *slipshoes*, a kind of loose slipper-like shoes. Upright decent people regarded such footwear as slovenly, and so the adjective came to be used more widely to refer to anything done in a sloppy thoughtless manner.

slogan

A *slogan* is a short phrase that is used in advertising a commercial product, making more widely known the message of a political party, etc. The word *slogan* comes from Scottish Gaelic *sluagh-ghairm*, army cry, from *sluagh*, army, and *gairm*, cry. The battle cries of the Scottish Gaelic soldiers were said to be the name of the clan or leader of the clan, repeated again and again by the soldiers in unison as they moved against the enemy. In due course the word came to describe any phrase used repeatedly in the promotion of a particular product or aim.

Other words from Scottish Gaelic that have become part of the English language include: *bard, cairn, clan,* and *loch.*

smog

Smog is a mixture of fog and smoke. The word was coined by a Dr H.A. des Voeux at a meeting of the Public Health Congress in 1905 to describe the smoky London fog. Examples of other blends include: *bit* from *bi*nary and dig*it*; *brunch* from *br*eakfast and l*unch*; *camcorder* from *cam*era and re*corder*; *motel* from *mo*tor and ho*tel*; and *transistor* from *trans*fer and resi*stor*.

soap opera

A *soap opera* or a *soap* is a popular television or radio serial about the daily lives of a group of people. This style of melodramatic drama derives its name from the fact that the sponsors of the first such programmes (on radio) in the USA were manufacturers of soap.

sock (*put a sock in it*)

The expression *put a sock in it* is used to tell someone to shut up. The phrase is said to derive from the days of the early wind-up gramophones, in which the sound emerged from a large horn. As the device had no volume control, those playing their records too loudly were told to *put a sock in it* – in other words literally to place a woollen sock inside the horn. Such an action would then muffle the troublesome level of noise.

sour grapes

The phrase *sour grapes* is used to refer to the bitterness felt when one pretends not to want something because one cannot have it oneself: *He said that the prize money wasn't important to him, but that was just sour grapes as he didn't win the competition.* The expression alludes to one of Aesop's fables, 'The Fox and the Grapes'. A fox is sitting below a mouth-watering bunch of grapes that are hanging above him. Unable to reach the grapes because they are too high, the fox tries to cover up his disappointment by murmuring to himself that the grapes are probably sour anyway.

sow the dragon's teeth; sow one's wild oats

The expression *sow the dragon's teeth* means to take a course of action that is intended to be peaceful, but in reality the course of action leads to dissension or warfare. The phrase alludes to Prince Cadmus in Greek mythology, who killed a dragon and planted its teeth. Later, a race of armed warriors sprang up from the teeth – they warred amongst themselves and only five escaped death. The phrase a *Cadmean victory*, a victory gained at an almost ruinous cost also derives from this story, the reference being to the victory of the five survivors in the struggle with other warriors.

If a young man *sows his wild oats*, he fritters his time away in worthless pleasure-seeking, particularly sexual activity before marriage: *He was a typical young man of his generation – sowed his wild oats for a few years and then settled down.* The expression refers to the wild oat, a wild grass or weed, so someone who sows wild oats is planting a crop that will bear no fruit and so is wasting his or her time.

spick-and-span

A room that is described as *spick and span* is extremely clean and tidy. The phrase comes ultimately from Old Norse *spānnýr*, absolutely new, from *spānn*, a chip of wood, and *nýr* new, referring to the newness of a chip of wood that had been freshly shaved. The word *spick*, spike, was added to the expression in the 16th century to give *spick-and-span-new*, which in time became shortened to *spick-and-span*, with the meaning 'trim or neat' coming in the mid-19th century.

spike someone's guns

To *spike someone's guns* means to prevent someone's plans from being fulfilled. The expression derives from the literal 'spiking' of muzzle-loading cannon. They could be put out of action by driving a spike, a pointed piece of metal, into the small hole through which the powder was ignited.

spill the beans

To *spill the beans* is to reveal a secret: *Why did you have to go and spill the beans about Ashley's party? It was meant to be a surprise!* The expression is said to go back to the ancient Greeks who held secret votes on the admission of new members into their secret societies. A white bean (standing for 'yes') or a black bean (standing for 'no') would be dropped into a jar. The beans were then counted in secrecy, but occasionally, so the story goes, the jar would be knocked over, spilling the beans – in other words, the secret would be out.

This story sounds attractive, but it has not been satisfactorily explained why the expression – if that is the true origin – entered the language only at the beginning of the 20th century.

spitting image

If someone is the *spitting image* of another person, he or she is exactly like that person: *He's the spitting image of Paul McCartney!* The expression derives from the phrase *spit and image*, from *spit*, as in *the very spit of* (e.g. *She's the very spit of her mother*) meaning exactly like. It is possible that *spit* is a shortened form of *spirit*, the original version of the phrase being the *spirit and image*.

spoil the ship for a ha'porth of tar

The expression *spoil the ship for a ha'porth of tar* means to render an entire project worthless by trying to avoid spending a little more money on something small but important. It is surprising that this idiomatic phrase has in fact no association with ships. The word *ship* was originally *sheep*, and the expression referred originally to the treatment of the sores of a sheep with a ha'porth (halfpenny's worth) of tar, to prevent the wound from getting worse. If one did not spend the small amount of money necessary to treat a sheep's sores, then the sheep might die.

spoke (put a spoke in someone's wheel)

To *put a spoke in someone's wheel* is to frustrate his or her activities or plans. It seems that the origin goes back to the time when carts had solid wheels. A *spoke* was a bar or pin that was inserted into a hole in the wheel and acted as a brake.

spree

A *spree* is a shortish period of unrestrained activity: *go on a spending spree*; *a drinking spree*. Sometimes the word is used to describe more violent activities, e.g. burglary or shooting. Such usage takes us back to the possible origin of the word, which is Scottish *spreath*, cattle raid.

square (back to square one)

Back to square one means that one has to start from the beginning again: *Rejecting the design for the new library has put the whole process back to square one.* The expression may derive from board games with numbers for each square, square one being the first. An alternative explanation refers to early soccer commentaries on radio, broadcast in Britain. Commentators used a plan of the field that was divided up into grids in order to locate the area of play for listeners. *Back to square one* meant that an attack had been successfully driven back to where it had begun.

steal someone's thunder

If someone *steals one's thunder*, they have pre-empted one in doing or saying something. The phrase goes back to the story of the critic and playwright John Dennis (1657–1734) who devised a backstage effect of thunder for his play *Appius and Virginia*, produced in 1709. The play was a failure, but the thunder effect that was made by shaking a sheet of tin was so successful that a few days later Dennis himself heard it in another theatre where *Macbeth* was being performed. Dennis' reaction to others' pirating his special effects was, 'See how the rascals use me! They will not let my play run, and yet they *steal my thunder*!'

stepchild

A *stepchild* is a child born of one's husband or wife by a previous marriage. The *step-* here has no association with a stage or 'step' in a family tree as though it referred to a further level of relationship. The word in fact comes from Old English *stēop-*, which in turn is derived from Old High German *stiufen*, to bereave. In other words, a *stepchild* was originally a bereaved

216

or orphaned child. In due course the word's meaning developed to cover the child of one's spouse by a former marriage.

sterling

British money is sometimes referred to as *sterling*: *£2000 sterling*. The origin of this word is Old English *steorling*, coin with a star on it, from Old English *steorra*, star and the diminutive suffix *-ling*. The allusion is to the small star which was embossed on an early Norman penny coin known as a *sterling*. When a larger currency unit became needed, it was taken as a pound of the smaller sterlings to give the pound *sterling*.

stop (pull out all the stops)

To *pull out all the stops* is to do all that is possible to achieve something: *They pulled out all the stops in order to get the project finished on time*. This idiomatic expression alludes to the organ. The stops on this musical instrument control the pipes which give the organ its wide range of tones. When all the stops have been pulled out, the organ gives its loudest, fullest sound.

straight from the horse's mouth

To hear information *straight from the horse's mouth* means that one hears it directly from the source – from the person who knows the truth. The phrase alludes to the traditional belief that the most reliable method of determining the age of a horse is to examine its teeth. So if one wanted to buy a horse, the best way of making sure that one was not being cheated by the salesman was to inspect the animal's teeth for oneself. See also *long in the tooth* (under LONG).

the straw that broke the camel's back

The expression *the straw that broke the camel's back* refers to an additional small burden that, coming after all others, proves to be too much to endure. The expression goes back to a phrase in *Dombey and Son* by Charles Dickens who wrote, 'As the last straw breaks the laden camel's back', but there was an earlier proverb, ''Tis the last feather that breaks the horse's back.' The full phrase *the straw that broke the camel's back* is often reduced to the form *the last* (or *final*) *straw*.

strike while the iron is hot

To *strike while the iron is hot* means that one acts at the most favourable time in order to get the best results: *You say the boss is in a good mood? You'd better strike while the iron is hot and ask him for your pay rise quickly!* The reference in the phrase was originally to the blacksmith's craft. Iron is most workable when white hot; the blacksmith had to *strike while the iron was hot* in order to form the right shape on the anvil, or he would have to heat up the iron again.

sure (as sure as eggs is eggs)

The simile *as sure as eggs is eggs* means 'certainly': *He'll be late again, as sure as eggs is eggs.* The expression almost certainly has nothing to do with eggs, but is an altered version of the mathematical 'x is x': something is as sure as x is x.

swallow (one swallow does not make a summer)

The saying *one swallow does not make a summer* means that one fortunate event does not necessarily mean that all one's difficulties are over or that a whole situation has improved. It is better to wait for additional proof before drawing conclusions. The expression dates back to Aristotle, in whose writings is recorded the phrase 'One swallow does not make a Spring.' The phrase alludes to the temperate swallows' migratory habits: all migrate to hot climates during winter. The return of just one swallow does not necessarily imply that summer has arrived.

swan song

A *swan song* is the farewell or final appearance of someone such as an actor or musician. The expression derives from the belief – found in the writings of the ancient Greeks and the poetry of Shakespeare and Coleridge, for instance – that a swan sings a beautiful sweet song just before it dies. The belief is in fact mistaken, but nevertheless the expression lingers.

swap horses in mid-stream

If someone *swaps* (or *changes*) *horses in mid-stream*, he or she suddenly changes the course of action being followed while the task is actually being undertaken. The expression was used by Abraham Lincoln, 'It is best not to swap horses while crossing the river,' in addressing the National Union League delegation in 1864. The League supported Lincoln's Republican nomination for a second term of office as US President. Lincoln was telling them that they should not choose him so much for his merits – many Republicans being dissatisfied with his conduct of the US Civil War – but rather because it would be a bad strategy for them to change leaders.

T

table (*turn the tables*)

To *turn the tables* is to cause a complete reversal in circumstances: *Having lost the first game, Harvey turned the tables on Jack in the next two and won the whole match.* The expression probably originally alludes to the reversing of the board in a game of chess or draughts to give each player an equal advantage. An alternative explanation suggests that the phrase goes back to the time when table-tops had two surfaces. One surface was kept smooth and polished and was used for eating and entertaining visitors. The other side was kept rough and was used as a work surface. So if you did not want to give a guest a warm reception, you turned the rough working surface uppermost.

taboo

A *taboo* is a prohibition on doing or saying something, especially if it is considered offensive or embarrassing: *For many people, death is still a taboo subject.* The word *taboo* has been borrowed from Tongan *tabu*, holy or untouchable, i.e. too holy to be touched.

tail (have one's tail between one's legs; turn tail)

If *you have your tail between your legs*, you feel defeated, ashamed, or dejected: *Thoroughly humiliated, he went off with his tail between his legs.* The expression goes back, according to some sources, to about 500 AD, when writers described frightened or cowardly dogs as having their tails between their legs. An animal that goes off with its tail between its legs *turns tail*, as another idiomatic expression has it – it turns round and runs away, because of defeat or fear.

talk nineteen to the dozen; talk turkey

If someone is *talking nineteen to the dozen*, he or she is talking away very fast. The expression is said to have originated in 18th-century Cornwall tin and copper mines, which were often affected by bad flooding. Steam-powered engines were used to pump water out of the mine shafts. It was worked out that the pumps were working at maximum load when they were pumping out 19,000 gallons of water for every 12 bushels of coal required to operate the engines – or 19 to the dozen.

To *talk turkey*, to talk seriously about business matters, is said to have this colourful origin. In colonial days, a white hunter and an Indian agreed that they would share equally the spoils of a day's hunting expedition. But, at the end of the day, when the time came to share the three crows and two turkeys, the white hunter divided the spoils unequally. He handed a crow to the Indian, giving himself a turkey, handed another crow to the Indian and the second turkey to himself. It was then that the Indian is said to have uttered the protest, 'You *talk* all *turkey* for you. Only talk crow for Indian.'

tally

A *tally* is a record or account, e.g. of how much money is spent or a score in a game: *Don't forget to keep a tally of everything that you spend.* The word derives ultimately from Latin *talea*, twig. Originally a tally was a stick that was scored with notches as a way of recording a business transaction. A wooden stick was notched with marks that represented numbers. It was then split down the middle through the notches so that each party had a record of the transaction and the amount owing or paid. When the debt was to be paid, the two pieces were put together. Tallies were used by the British royal exchequer up to the 18th century. After the practice had been discontinued, the tallies were burnt at the House of Lords in 1834, causing such a fire that it set fire to the old Houses of Parliament.

tantalize

If one *tantalizes* someone, one teases him or her by offering something pleasant only to disappoint him or her by withholding it. The word derives from Greek mythology. *Tantalus*, the mythical King of Phrygia, was punished for offences against the gods. In Hades he was condemned to stand in water that receded whenever he tried to drink it and under branches of fruit that moved away whenever he tried to grasp them.

tawdry

Something that is *tawdry* is cheap and showy. The word comes from the name of the queen of Northumbria St *Audrey* (Ethelrida; died 679). In olden times a fair was held annually on 17 October in her honour. The fair was noted for its good-quality jewellery and fine silk scarves, which in time came to be known as *St Audrey's laces*. Later, however, the fine scarves were replaced by cheap, gaudy imitations and so the word *tawdry* developed, a shortening and alteration of (Sain)*t Audrey*('s laces), a term that is now applied to anything that is cheap, showy, or of poor quality.

teetotal

Someone who is *teetotal* never drinks any alcohol. The word is said to have been coined in 1833 by the English advocate of total abstinence from alcohol, Richard Turner (died 1846). (Interestingly, the adverb *teetotally* is said to have been used in America from 1807 onwards.) Turner was one of the founder members of the Total Abstinence Society, formed in Preston, England on 22 March 1832. It seems likely that the word was coined to emphasize the significance of *total*: *T* (hence *tee*) for *total* abstinence.

tenterhooks (on tenterhooks)

To be *on tenterhooks* is to be tense and anxious about something that is going to happen: *All the students are on tenterhooks, with the exam results due this week.* The expression refers to the former process of stretching freshly woven cloth. The material was dried and stretched on a framework (a *tenter*), and held taut by small hooks known as *tenterhooks*. From this literal tension developed the figurative sense of being in a state of anxiety or suspense.

throw in the towel/sponge

If someone *throws in the towel* (or *sponge*), he or she acknowledges or admits defeat and gives up an attempt to do something: *It's a bit early to throw in the towel, isn't it? You only started work on the project last week!* The expression derives from boxing. A boxer's second will throw in the towel or sponge, so disqualifying the boxer. This action is therefore a sign of surrender and an acknowledgement of defeat.

tilt at windmills

The expression *tilt at windmills* means to attack imaginary enemies in the belief that they are real. This idiomatic phrase comes from the novel *Don Quixote de la Mancha* by the Spanish novelist Miguel de Cervantes Saavedra (1547–1616). On his travels through the countryside, Don Quixote attacks some windmills, thinking that they are evil giants, which he, as a chivalrous knight, is bound to fight. He charges at them, with extended lance, only for his lance to get caught in one of the windmill's sails, lifting him into the air, sending him tumbling to the ground, and injuring him.

tinker's cuss/dam

The phrase *tinker's cuss* (or *dam* or *damn*) is used to refer to the smallest amount or extent of consideration: *I wouldn't give a tinker's damn what she thinks.* The expression probably originally referred to the reputation of tinkers. These itinerant menders of pots and pans were held in low esteem and since they allegedly swore so much, one of their cusses (curses) would be of little value. An alternative explanation alludes originally to the *dam*, a small piece of bread or clay that was used by tinkers to keep solder in place while they were mending pots and pans. Once a hole had been repaired, the dam was worthless, and was thrown away.

tit for tat

The expression *tit for tat* means an equivalent act of retaliation: *Sarah took Jason's colouring pens, so Jason took her painting book. It was tit for tat.* The phrase is an alteration of the 16th-century expression *tip for tap*, the word *tip* at that time meaning 'blow', so this expression literally means 'blow for blow'.

toady

A *toady* is someone who flatters people in the hope of gaining favours from them. The word is a shortening of *toadeater*, the name of the assistant of a travelling charlatan doctor. The 'doctor' employed a toadeater who appeared to swallow a toad, which was in those days considered poisonous. The toadeater would then take the antidote offered by his master, and would be dramatically cured. On the basis of such remarkable medicine, the doctor would then attempt to sell his potions to any crowd that might have gathered.

toast

To drink a *toast* to someone is to wish that person good health, success, etc., and then drink some wine or other alcoholic drink in his or her honour. The use of the word *toast* in this sense goes back to the former practice of adding a piece of spiced toast to a glass or tankard. This had the effect of improving the drink and also served to collect sediment at the bottom. In the course of time, the word *toast* came to be applied to the drink itself.

Topsy (like Topsy, it just growed)

If something is said to be *like Topsy, it just grew*, it has come from an unknown origin and has developed by itself. The expression is based on the following exchange in the novel *Uncle Tom's Cabin* by Harriet Beecher Stowe (1852): 'Where were you born?' 'Never was born!' persisted Topsy ... 'Do you know who made you?' 'Nobody, as I knows on,' said the child, with a short laugh ... 'I spect I *grow'd*. Don't think nobody ever made me.'

treacle

Treacle is an example of a word with a surprising origin. *Treacle* is a dark, thick, and sticky syrup that is produced when sugar is refined. But the word derives ultimately from Greek *thēr*, which means 'a wild animal'. What is the connection? If a wild animal bit someone, an antidote was needed to counteract the effects of the poisonous bite. The ancients believed that this antidote lay in the flesh of the animal itself, and so coined the word *thēriakē*, an antidote to a poisonous bite, from *thēr*. The word came via Latin into Middle English as *triacle*, which referred to a sweetened medicinal compound used especially as an antidote to poison. Gradually, the word *treacle* came to be used to refer to the sweetening agent itself.

trip the light fantastic

The expression *trip the light fantastic* means to dance. The phrase derives from John Milton's poem *L'Allegro* (1632):

> Sport that wrinkled Care derides,
> And Laughter holding both his sides.
> Come, and trip it as ye go
> On the light fantastic toe.

Trojan horse

A *Trojan horse* is something that is intended to subvert or defeat from within: a disguised way of introducing something dangerous or harmful. The expression refers to the defeat by the Greeks of the city of Troy by presenting to the city a large wooden horse. The horse was accepted by the city, whereupon the Greek warriors hidden inside it emerged to launch their victorious assault on Troy.

U

umbrella

An *umbrella* is a portable device with a stick and a cloth-covered frame that is used as a protection from the rain. The word derives from Italian *ombrella*, from Latin *umbra*, shade. The original umbrellas did not serve as protection from the rain, but as a screen from the sun. We now only use *parasol* in this sense.

utopia

A *utopia* is an imaginary, ideal, and perfect place. The word was originally the title of a Latin book, published in 1516, by the English statesman and scholar Sir Thomas More (1478–1535). In *Utopia*, More described an imaginary island of this same name with a perfect social, political, economic, and legal system. More coined the word from the Greek words *ou*, not and *topos*, place, and so according to its Greek origin, a utopia does not really exist, but is purely imaginary, since *utopia* means 'nowhere'.

V

vaccine

A *vaccine* is a preparation of micro-organisms designed to protect the body from a particular disease by stimulating the production of antibodies. The word *vaccine*, from Latin *vacca*, cow, entered the language at the end of the 18th century when the British physician Edward Jenner (1749–1823) noted how someone who had caught cowpox was immune to the disease of smallpox. So someone who was inoculated with the vaccine of the cowpox virus would develop antibodies against smallpox and become immune to this disease. In time the word *vaccine* came to be used to refer to preparations administered to provide immunity to other diseases.

vandal

A *vandal* is someone who deliberately destroys or damages property. The word derives from the *Vandals*, the Germanic people, who moved southwards from Scandinavia in the first four centuries AD, overrunning Gaul, Spain, and North Africa in the fifth century and sacking Rome in 455. The devastation that they caused was so severe that their name has ever since stood for those who bring about wanton destruction.

vaudeville

The variety entertainment known as *vaudeville* derives from Middle French *vaudevire*, popular satirical song. This in turn is a shorter version of the expression *chanson du vau-de-Vire*, song of the valley of *Vire*, the *Vire* being the name of a river in Normandy in north-west France. Originally, it seems, a certain fuller of this valley, Olivier Basselin in the 15th century, wrote poems and drinking songs. It was from such songs that the popular satirical verses – and eventually the theatrical light entertainment known as *vaudeville* – developed.

ventriloquism

Ventriloquism is the art of producing speech sounds that seem to come from a source other than the speaker's vocal organs. Often a ventriloquist has a dummy which is manipulated by the speaker to open its mouth and move its limbs. The origin of the word *ventriloquism* is a combination of two Latin words: *venter*, belly, and *loqui*, to speak. It was generally thought that since the origin of the sound was not the mouth, the sound had to come from the ventriloquist's belly.

vermicelli

Vermicelli is pasta in the form of long thin threads which are smaller in diameter than spaghetti. The word is the plural of Italian *vermicello* and literally means 'little worms'. If the thought of eating a plate of worms is unappetizing, try a dish of unravelled *spaghetti* instead. *Spaghetti* is the plural of Italian *spaghetto* and literally means 'little strings or cords'.

villain

A *villain* is a scoundrel or criminal: a person who does evil. The word has not always been used in a derogatory sense, however. The word comes from the Medieval Latin *villanus* and meant simply 'a worker on a *villa*, a country estate'. In feudal England a *villein* was a lord's serf.

Other examples of words that have gained a negative sense include: *crafty*, once meaning 'strong; skilful', now meaning 'cunning'; *notorious*, once meaning 'well known', now meaning 'well known for something unfavourable'; *pedant*, once meaning 'schoolmaster', now meaning 'someone concerned with small unimportant details'; *vulgar*, once meaning 'ordinary; pertaining to the common people', now meaning 'indecent'.

vitamin

A *vitamin* is an organic compound which is essential for maintaining healthy life and growth in animals. The word was originally coined by the US biochemist Casimir Funk (1884–1967) in 1912. The word was originally spelt *vitamine* by Funk, from a combination of two Latin words, *vita*, life, and *amine*, from the belief that it contained amino acid. When it was later found that amino acids were not present in vitamins, the *e* was dropped.

viz

The written abbreviation *viz*, meaning namely, is used to introduce specific examples. The word *viz* is itself a shortening of Latin *videlicet*, one is permitted to see, from *vidēre*, to see, and *licet*, it is permitted. The final *z* of *viz* is in fact a changed form of the number *3*, which was used by monks in medieval times to show a contraction.

The abbreviation *viz* is used only in writing; when read aloud, it is normally rendered as *namely* or *that is to say*.

W

wagon (*on the wagon*)

To be *on the wagon* is to abstain from drinking alcohol. The original version of this phrase was *on the water-cart*. During the late 19th century, horse-drawn water carts wetted down the dry dusty roads of summer. People in the 1890s began to speak of climbing aboard the water-cart, in their attempts to avoid strong drink. Thus came the expression *I'm on the water-cart*, meaning 'I'm trying to stop drinking,' first recorded in 1901 in *Mrs Wiggs of the Cabbage Patch* (1901). *Wagon* soon replaced *cart* in the phrase and in time the expression became shortened to *on the wagon*.

warm the cockles of one's heart

If something *warms the cockles of one's heart*, it makes one feel very pleased and happy: *It really warms the cockles of my heart to hear a story like that!* In this expression, the chambers of the heart are likened to cockleshells. So these chambers, the ventricles, were called *cockles*, and represented the innermost depths of one's being and seat of affections and emotions.

warpath (on the warpath)

If someone is *on the warpath,* he or she is angrily getting ready for a fight: *The health unions are on the warpath. They are gearing themselves up for battle following threatened redundancies among their members.* The expression originally referred to the route taken by North American Indians going on a warlike expedition or going to war.

warts and all

The phrase *warts and all* is used to refer to a complete description that does not attempt to hide any faults or defects: *a warts-and-all report on life in our schools today.* The expression is based on the instruction by the English statesman Oliver Cromwell to the portrait painter Sir Peter Lely: 'Mr Lely, I desire you would use all your skill to paint my picture truly like me, and not flatter me at all; but remark all these roughnesses, pimples, warts, and everything as you see me, otherwise I will never pay a farthing for it.'

wash one's hands of something

To *wash one's hands of something* is to disclaim all responsibility for it: *I wash my hands of the whole affair. If you want to be involved further, then that's up to you.* This expression has its origins in the Authorized (King James) Version of the Bible, Matthew 27:24: 'When Pilate saw that he could prevail nothing, but that rather a tumult was made, he took water, and washed his hands before the multitude, saying, I am innocent of the blood of this just person: see ye to it.' Pontius Pilate washed his hands, symbolizing his dissociation from the people's desire to crucify Jesus.

wedlock

Wedlock is an old-fashioned word for the state of being married. The *lock* in this word has nothing to do with the 'closed bonds' of marriage, as may be thought, but is simply derived from the Old English suffix *-lāc*, used to denote activity. (Interestingly, this suffix survives only in the word *wedlock*.) Old English *wedd* meant a pledge or security of any kind, so *wedlock* was originally the action of giving pledges, in particular, the giving of marriage vows.

Welsh rabbit

Welsh rabbit was the original name of the dish of melted cheese on toast. The name was coined with the humorous allusion to the fact that only the very rich could afford to eat game. So ordinary people only seldom had the opportunity of tasting rabbit. With wry humour, cheese on toast – a dish that ordinary people could afford – was therefore described as their *Welsh rabbit*.

Later, the name was artificially changed by some to give the affected form *Welsh rarebit*.

whipping boy

A *whipping boy* is a scapegoat – someone who is made to bear the blame for others' mistakes, particularly someone unimportant who is blamed for his or her superior's errors. The expression derives from a practice that was common amongst European royalty four or five centuries ago. A prince was educated alongside a boy commoner, with the commoner being punished instead of the young prince every time that the latter deserved it. For example, Edward (later Edward VI), the son of Henry VIII, had the whipping boy Barnaby Fitzpatrick who was beaten whenever the punishment was due to

Edward. However, while Edward died of consumption at 16, Fitzpatrick, it is said, lived to a relatively old age.

white elephant

A *white elephant* is something expensive but unwanted and useless: *With the recession, planners now fear that the new shopping centre will turn out to be a huge white elephant.* The phrase alludes to the former tradition in Thailand where rare white (albino) elephants became, when born or caught, the property of the king. He alone had the right to ride or use such sacred animals. When one of the courtiers fell out of the king's favour, the king would show his displeasure by making a gift of one of the white elephants to the courtier. The courtier would be ruined: the white elephant not only proved immensely costly to keep but also could not be put to work – hence the present meaning of the expression.

Whitsun

Whitsun is the Christian festival, at the seventh Sunday after Easter, that celebrates the coming of the Holy Spirit at Pentecost. The term comes from Old English *hwīta sunnandæg*, white Sunday. The Sunday was known as *white* probably from the white robes traditionally worn by those being baptized, who were numerous at this time of year.

The day following *Whit Sunday* was formerly a bank holiday (*Whit Monday*) and this term is still sometimes unofficially used for the bank holiday that falls on the last Monday of May, known officially as Spring Bank Holiday.

wig

A *wig* is an artificial covering of hair for the head. The word is a 17th-century shortening of *periwig*, which itself comes from *peruke*, via French, from Old Italian *parrucca*.

Two other derived words probably come from *wig*: first, a *bigwig*, an important person – from the 18th-century idea that the more important the man, the larger the wig he would wear. Secondly, to give someone a good *wigging*, to rebuke him or her sharply, comes from the fact that the person who was meting out the criticism would have been someone in authority, and so someone who wore a wig.

win one's spurs

To *win one's spurs* is to gain honour and recognition by proving one's ability in a particular field: *Don't you think you should let him win his spurs before we promote him to manager?* The expression alludes to medieval times when a young squire or prince performed his first distinguished brave achievement. He would be honoured by being dubbed a knight by his lord and presented with a pair of gilded spurs.

wind (take the wind out of someone's sails)

To *take the wind out of someone's sails* is to reduce that person's sense of self-confidence, especially by suddenly doing something that places him or her at a disadvantage: *She really took the wind out of my sails by telling me she'd been offered the job – I thought they were going to give it to me.* The expression alludes to one ship sailing so near to another on the windward side that the latter is deprived of wind and lacks the power to move.

a wolf in sheep's clothing

The expression *a wolf in sheep's clothing* is used to refer to someone who appears to be friendly and harmless but in reality is cruel and dangerous. The phrase derives from the words of Jesus, as recorded in the Sermon on the Mount (Matthew 7:15): 'Beware of false prophets, which come to you in sheep's clothing, but inwardly they are ravening wolves.'

woman

The word for a *woman*, an adult female human being, comes from *wifman*, a combination of two Old English words, *wif*, woman or wife (from which we get *wife*), and *mann*, human being. In time, *wifman* became *wimman* (plural *wimmen*, hence the pronunciation of our modern plural form *women*), and later *woman*.

wood (touch/knock on wood)

Touch wood (American equivalent *knock on wood*) is a superstitious phrase often said simultaneously with touching a piece of wood. It expresses a desire to prevent bad luck and to gain fortune or good luck: *So far, I've had no expensive repairs to do to the house, touch wood.* There are various explanations of the origin of this practice. The custom may go back to ancient times when it was believed that trees contained friendly guardian spirits. To touch a tree was therefore to appeal for good luck. An alternative theory is that the practice refers to a chasing game: those who touch wood are safe from capture. A third suggestion is that the wood may have referred originally to a crucifix or rosary beads. To touch these would be to seek divine protection.

wool (pull the wool over someone's eyes)

If one *pulls the wool over someone's eyes* one deceives him or her in order to gain an advantage: *The government is trying to stop misleading guarantees, short measures, and other methods of pulling the wool over the consumers' eyes.* This idiomatic expression goes back to the time when wigs were commonly worn by gentlemen. *Wool* was a humorous term for hair or a wig. The origin of the phrase may lie in the law-courts. It may be that when a judge's wig slipped down over his eyes, a clever barrister who had tricked the judge joked that he had *pulled the wool over the judge's eyes.* Or, more simply, if someone pulled a gentleman's wig down over his eyes he would be unable to notice what was happening around him: he would be easy to deceive.

the world is my oyster

The saying *the world is one's oyster* means that one thinks that one is fortunate enough to do whatever one wants or to go to wherever one wants: *'You're young; you're rich – the possibilities are endless, young man! Enjoy life while you can! The world is your oyster.'* The phrase comes from Shakespeare's *The Merry Wives of Windsor* (Act 2, Scene ii):

Why, then the world's mine oyster,
Which I with sword will open.

the writing on the wall

The expression *the writing is on the wall* means that there are signs that warn of imminent collapse or failure: *The writing's been on the wall for a few weeks now and it's doubtful if the business will last another three months.* The phrase refers to the mysterious inscription that appeared on the wall of the royal palace of King Belshazzar, interpreted as warning of the king's downfall, as recorded in the biblical book of Daniel, chapter 5.

X

Xmas

Xmas is an informal word for *Christmas*: *Merry Xmas everyone!*
The *X* was originally the Greek letter *chi*, written like a capital
X. This was the first letter of the Greek form of *Christ* and has
long been used as an abbreviation for this name.

Y

ye

The archaic *ye*, meaning 'the', as in the fanciful *Ye Olde Teashoppe*, has nothing to do with the *ye* meaning 'you', as may be thought. It was in fact an erroneous rendering of an Old English form. In Old English the single letter **þ**, known as thorn, was equivalent to our modern *th*. In time, however, this unfamiliar letter was often misrepresented as *Y*, to give *ye* for *the* and hence the pseudo-archaic signs that woo tourists.

yuppie

The word *yuppie* is an Americanism that came into frequent use in Britain in the mid-1980s. The word is derived from *y*oung *u*rban (or *u*pwardly mobile) *p*rofessional and the suffix -*ie*.

INDEX

diagnosis, 40
dickens, what, how, etc, the, 77
die is cast, the, 77
diesel, 78
dilemma, 115
dilly-dilly, 64
ding-dong, 64
dinghy, 39
dirge, 78
dismal, 78
distaff, 79
do as you would be done by, 79
Doctor Livingstone, I presume, 79
dog in the manger, a, 80; dog days, 80
doldrums, in the doldrums, 80
dollar, 80
double Dutch, 83
doubt, 74
doubting Thomas, a, 81
draconian, 81
dramatis personae, 174
dressed to the nines, 81
drop in the ocean, a, 82
duffel, 82
dunce, 82
dungarees, 39, 83
Dunkirk spirit, the, 83
Dutch, 83; Dutch courage, 83; Dutch treat, 83; go Dutch, 84; Dutch uncle, 84
dyed in the wool, 84

E
earmark, 85
earwig, 85
easel, 85
Easter, 86
eat humble pie, 86
eavesdropper, 87
eccentric, 87
edit, 40
editor, 40
electricity, 87

elementary, my dear Watson, 88
eleven, at the eleventh hour, 88
ell, 118
end, make ends meet, 88
engrossing, 152
enthusiast, 89
Epsom salts, 89
errant, 9
Esq., 89
esquire, 89
etiquette, 90
eureka, 90
exchequer, 91
excruciating, 91
explode, 91
eye, an eye for an eye, 92

F
face the music, 93
farce, 93
fast, play fast and loose with someone, 94
feather, feather in one's cap, a, 94; feather one's nest, 94
fell, at one fell swoop, 95
fiddle while Rome burns, 95
fifth column, 95
filibuster, 96
final straw, the, 218
fine kettle of fish, a, 96
flagstone, 97
flash in the pan, a, 97
flu, 119
fly in the ointment, a, 97
foolscap, 98
foot, have one foot in the grave, 98
forcemeat, 93
forlorn hope, 98
freelance, 99
from pillar to post, 175

G
galore, 133
game isn't worth the candle, the, 100